NE ME QUITTE PAS

SINGLES ▲ A SERIES EDITED BY JOSHUA CLOVER AND EMILY J. LORDI

NE ME QUITTE PAS

MAYA ANGELA SMITH

DUKE UNIVERSITY PRESS DURHAM AND LONDON 2025

Printed in the United States of America on acid-free paper ∞

Project Editor: Lisa Lawley

Designed by Matthew Tauch

Typeset in Bitter and Work Sans by Copperline Book Services

Library of Congress Cataloging-in-Publication Data

Names: Smith, Maya Angela, author.

Title: Ne me quitte pas / Maya Angela Smith.

Other titles: Singles (Duke University Press)

Description: Durham : Duke University Press, 2025. | Series: Singles |
Includes bibliographical references and index.

Identifiers: LCCN 2024028361 (print)

LCCN 2024028362 (ebook)

ISBN 9781478031468 (paperback)

ISBN 9781478028253 (hardcover)

ISBN 9781478060444 (ebook)

Subjects: LCSH: Brel, Jacques. Ne me quitte pas. | Brel, Jacques—
Criticism and interpretation. | Popular music—Social aspects—
History—20th century. | Cover versions—History and criticism. |
Songs—Analysis, appreciation.

Classification: LCC ML410.B8433 S65 2025 (print) |
LCC ML410.B8433 (ebook) | DDC 782.42164—dc23/eng/20241118

LC record available at https://lccn.loc.gov/2024028361

LC ebook record available at https://lccn.loc.gov/2024028362

For Amar'e

CONTENTS

Intro

"NE ME QUITTE PAS." Those words meant nothing to sixteen-year-old me, and yet they meant everything. Staccato sounds, foreign and strange, enveloped in a voice that felt like home.

From the moment I discovered Nina Simone in my parents' record collection, I knew no performer would ever move me more. It wasn't just the richness of her unique voice or the emotion that hung on each note. It wasn't just the majestic way she drew life from eighty-eight keys, her ardent commitment to civil rights, or her inspiring deeds interspersed throughout the stories my parents told of their upbringing in the American South. It was also the way she gave me permission to claim my own voice, which found freedom not in my native tongue, but in French.

I credit this song as one of the reasons I, a Black American woman from a monolingual, English-speaking family, studied French in college. And it was Nina who made sure I kept with it when the whitewashed curriculum of my textbooks suggested French was a language only for white people. Each time I experienced alienation or frustration in my studies—over the difficulty of pronouncing French and memorizing its complex rules, over being the only Black student in my courses—I would play Nina and become emboldened by the French that hovered on her lips. This sonic talisman saw me through my linguistic journey and led me to Paris, a much Blacker space than I had ever imagined. It even wielded the power to guide my educational and professional journey to become a French professor.

"Ne me quitte pas" (Don't leave me) has traveled its own winding road, from its inception and original performances to its numerous covers, translations, and adaptations. In 1959, before he was a household name, Belgian singer-songwriter Jacques Brel wrote and performed this visceral and haunting plea. I remember encountering Brel's original in a college classroom and being instructed to use my burgeoning language abilities to analyze the lyrics. I was no longer relying solely on my body's response to Nina's voice and artistry to connect with the song. I could now also lose myself in the intricacies of the words and the poetic images they conveyed. Beginning to understand the lyrics and learning the conditions in which Brel wrote them changed my relationship to the song.

I spent the next couple of decades waffling about whether Simone's or Brel's version spoke to me more. Brel's provides intrigue, supposedly the product of a failed extramarital affair. His over-the-top performance sells the song's heartache, making me question where the line falls between the autobiographical lived experience of a person using art to cope with loss and the convincing portrayal of pain by an artist telling an invented story through song. Meanwhile, I wonder how my deep respect and admiration for Nina colors how I engage with "Ne me quitte pas." Now that I know her version is a cover, am I so quick to believe the song is hers? At the same time, I see myself in her Blackness, her womanness, her Americanness, which makes her version vibrate within me in ways Brel's does not. It makes it mine.

Then there is Shirley Bassey's performance of Rod McKuen's English translation, "If You Go Away," first introduced to me by a friend. I admit, my mother tongue sounds strange in a song I mainly associate with French. Many critics argue that the translation doesn't do the original justice. Is it the questionable translation that severs the song's hold over me, or does Bassey's larger-than-life pageantry mute the heartfelt emotions Brel and Simone stir? At the same time, Bassey's evocative vocals and regal stature entreat new feelings to the surface. Much is lost, much is gained.

Just when I had started to make sense of the different emotional resonances of each version, a colleague told me to listen to Sasha Velour's drag performance of "If I Go Away." By lip-syncing Bassey, Velour takes her theatrics to a new level. While there's a subtle disconnect between the French and English lyrics, it's the violence of Velour's performance that upends the song's affective qualities, transforming a love song into a spectacle of horror. Encountering Velour led me down a rabbit hole of multiple adaptations of "Ne me quitte pas," each serving different artistic purposes and evoking distinctive emotions.

For years I've sat with, sung with, and tapped into complex emotions with "Ne me quitte pas." It has been in the background as I write. It has been in the foreground as I dance. It has been a through line as I studied and worked toward my professional goals. And now, a song Nina gifted to my eager ears decades ago has become the central object of a book. I get to analyze this song as a text, as a piece of cultural production written in a specific context, and as a work of mass/popular art that travels, being reinterpreted and recontextualized in numerous ways. A meditation on translation in the most expansive meaning of the word, this book explores how "Ne me quitte pas" travels across languages, geographies, genres, and generations. How does this song make manifest the experience of translation, seen through the Latin *trans* + *latio*, or the idea of being carried across? How does it shift, refract, and change through the processes of covering, translating, and adaptating? What does it indicate about the choices translators of song make and how they differ from considerations in literary translation? What can an analysis of language, sound, emotion, culture, gender, and race tell us about the impact a song has on its audiences and on music scholarship? How do the ways we read this song shed light on various aesthetic, social, and political values, both historically and in the present day? What makes this song so translatable and therefore viral (something it achieved before being viral was even a thing)?

A song's power ultimately derives from its effect on the listener. Therefore, this book explores "Ne me quitte pas" by privileging audience experiences, from contemporary music criticism to journalistic retrospectives to scholarly interventions to YouTube commentary. And since a song's impact is very much situated in the body, I also reflect on my own embodied experience and sense of self—a useful tool to think through issues of (auto)biography, authenticity, and emotional truthfulness. Finally, because "Ne me quitte pas" set me on the path to becoming a professor and has been an object of analysis in my courses on language, culture, and identity, I've also interspersed throughout these pages my students' experiences with the song.

Nina Simone became my hero because of how she unapologetically moved through the world, refusing to accept the limitations others placed on her. She leveraged her classical music training to force audiences to reimagine what Black musicians could do. She used her songwriting skills and platform to implore audiences to question the inhumane treatment of Black people in the US and abroad. But it was her singing in French that had the most substantive effect on me because it showed me how to cross borders I once thought insurmountable. Her "Ne me quitte pas" pushed me to learn French with all its challenges and to encounter a new world that had seemed out of reach. I call on Nina again to guide me in this book's meditative journey of crossing disciplinary boundaries as I rely on francophone studies, music studies, linguistics, translation theory, adaptation studies, affect theory, race and ethnicity studies, and gender studies to tell the story of "Ne me quitte pas," how it travels, the myriad ways humans interact with the song, and the artistic and cultural significance of the performances surrounding it.

The Singles series is about singles—discrete musical tracks of great personal or social significance that are distributed to and heard by millions. I have taken some liberty with this assignment by not focusing on one singular version. Instead, I am using a single as a jumping off point to delve into a song where each version (Brel's, Simone's, Bassey's) has long-lasting, mass appeal, often to completely separate audiences. I am therefore grateful to have been given this space to reflect on the ways these different singles make "Ne me quitte pas" into an exceptional work of art. Each single has a story to tell about the impact it has on millions of people, including the artists who perform and record it. As such, "Ne me quitte pas" and its various iterations exist for me not as discrete art objects, but as a constellation of cultural production that actively influences how I feel and who I am.

▶ 01 "Ne me quitte pas"

Jacques Brel Composes the

Ultimate Breakup Song

ANYONE WHO HAS WATCHED a live recording of Brel singing "Ne me quitte pas" knows the viewing experience is almost transcendent. The version he performed on November 10, 1966, at Maison de Radio France (archived by INA, France's National Audiovisual Institute) has a particularly mesmerizing effect.[1] In the video recording of the performance, the camera closes in on Brel's face so tightly it cuts off his chin and hairline, making the viewer feel as if they could dab the sweat off his brow. This framing draws attention to every eye twitch, lip quiver, and nostril flare, bolstering our emotional connection to Brel as he bares his soul to the listener. Those who speak French experience how poetic heartbreak can be, and even those who don't understand the lyrics can tell from the song's melody, its orchestration, and Brel's performance that it's one of the saddest ever written. But how did this song come to be? Why is it so effective at conveying intense emotions? What is the sonic journey we experience as spectators when we listen to it? And what does all this say about the worlds in which the song exists?

Contextualizing Chanson

Chanson française is a genre of popular music that has existed since the Middle Ages, with the *chanson de geste*, and has been adapted to fit the expectations of different eras. Modern chanson emerged at the turn of the twentieth century and reached international acclaim through cabarets and music halls. The 1930s saw performers such as Charles Trenet and Édith Piaf become major stars both domestically and internationally. The 1950s, when Brel began his career, represented a more sophisticated style of music, with the ascendency of singer-songwriters such as Léo Ferré, Georges Brassens, and Brel himself.[2] While chanson is viewed as literary, cultured, and poetic, it's also an expression of popular culture and attuned to everyday life.

The figure of the singer-songwriter was central to the genre's success, and Brel was particularly adept at integrating the seemingly competing objectives of high-class notions of art and popular sentiment. Known as a *prêtre-ouvrier* (worker-priest)—a nod to his Catholic upbringing and ability to convey the lived experiences of laborers—Brel brought a literary sensibility to working-class music: "He didn't enjoy the idea of being the darling of Parisian sophisticates.... He wanted his work to belong to the people ('I never sing for audiences; I sing for people')."[3] Brel harnessed the power of language to imbue listeners with a sense of ownership of the human experiences he wrote about.

France and parts of the francophone world accord social prestige to literature and mastery of the French language.[4] A singer-songwriter embodies Frenchness and transmits French and francophone culture through language. While a relationship to a high register of language might appear elitist to outsiders, in French and francophone contexts it's integral to a wider cultural identity and even described as a uniquely French cultural trait.[5] Born into a French-speaking Flemish family on the outskirts of Brussels, Brel excelled in French throughout his schooling, particularly in reading and writing.[6] Thus, from an early age, he honed the sophisticated use of French that audiences expected from chanson artists.

At the same time, singer-songwriters are more than word-smiths. Orality takes center stage as they, the interpreters of their own texts, must convincingly bring these words to life. Brel has been lauded for his theatricality and his unique stage presence.[7] As with French, he showed a propensity for acting since childhood.[8] He became the quintessential performer who died with his words, sang with his face and whole body, and made his texts come alive by erasing possible written imperfections.[9] Brel achieved chanson's remit of representing the finest that written and spoken language can offer.

Brel's success can also be attributed to the role of the state in developing and perpetuating French identity. With the establishment of the Ministry of Culture in 1959, headed by André Malraux, the French government defined and disseminated Frenchness through the protection of various art forms.[10] Malraux conceived his mission as bringing France's brilliant cultural heritage to the widest audience possible.[11] French media, particularly radio and television, promoted this notion of French exceptionalism—the way France stands apart from the rest of Europe and the world with regard to culture. In Brel's heyday, chanson was considered the pinnacle of French musical expression. Radio programming was often recorded in French music halls, such as the Olympia, where Brel amassed his popularity. The rise of variety shows, which closely followed the music hall–inspired radio format, continued this tradition but in a visual medium.[12] The variety show *Discorama* (1959–75), a mix of interviews and musical performances, was instrumental in bringing Brel and his sweaty, engrossing performances to audiences across France on the only television channel that existed at the time, state-controlled Channel 1.[13] Because of the lack of radio stations and television channels, and the fact that most were run by the state until the 1980s, the French government could control what hit the airwaves, protecting the interests of the French music industry from foreign competition and dictating what was considered important cultural content.[14] With its focus on elevated language and French cultural sensibilities, chanson reflected back to a French audience the image they strived to achieve.

Paradoxically, Brel himself wasn't French. How then could he exemplify an identity category he did not inhabit? It was through the creation of this song and his convincing performance that he embodied the exceptionalism of French art. Brel achieved what many would consider as artistic perfection through his extraordinary use of language and his ability to make listeners feel. In other words, there is something in the art that allows for *trans + latio*, for being carried across national borders to claim Frenchness. And from a practical standpoint, the recordings—both the album version and his 1966 on-air performance—ensured that Brel's voice and face would enter homes across France and even the world.

Music as an Autobiographical Journey

In the foreword to *Jacques Brel en 40 chansons*, which analyzes Brel's music through a biographical lens, Stéphane Loisy portrays Brel not as a destination, but as a journey—the quest for absolute passion that buckles under the pain of mediocrity.[15] No song better exemplifies that tortured journey than "Ne me quitte pas," described as an ode to romantic despair that became a major work of French cultural heritage. Brel found singing about love to be relatively banal. As Loisy shows, Brel was more interested in how love dies because that's where poetry lives.[16]

While musical texts are usually considered works of fiction, story elements in fictional texts often emerge from reference to "more or less reliable documented evidence of past events."[17] In other words, real life influences artistic production. But to what extent is that true of "Ne me quitte pas"?

Here are the facts. The married Brel had a well-documented affair with fellow performer Suzanne "Zizou" Gabriello for several years. In addition to being his lover and colleague, Gabriello was instrumental in convincing Brel to evolve his music hall persona to become a singer of serious love songs.[18] After reading an article that depicted Brel as a happy family man, Gabriello realized he would never divorce his wife, Thérèse "Miche" Michielsen, and so ended the affair.[19] A few months later, "Ne me quitte pas" was released, a song of groveling, begging a lover to come back by promising the impossible.

Loisy presents Brel's music as an autobiographical testimony of his life and implies we should read his songs as conveying the truth Brel lived.[20] But who is the addressee of "Ne me quitte pas"? Loisy argues that those who believe it's Gabriello fail to grapple with the paradoxes and contradictions inherent in Brel's love life. It's possible the song was a way for Brel to assuage the guilt he felt for his extramarital affairs, making "Ne me quitte pas" a plea to his wife to not quit on their relationship.[21] But it is not surprising that Loisy would advance an interpretation that prioritizes the wife over the mistress, given that he coedited *Brel en 40 chansons* with Brel's nephew Bruno Brel. Importantly, Jacques

Brel denies any autobiographic intent, calling "Ne me quitte pas" the song of a coward who bends under grief without stipulating that he was indeed this coward.[22]

Brel was socialized as a chanson artist, and "Ne me quitte pas" is in many ways a consummate example of chanson artistry. As such, he could simply be playing the part instead of divulging autobiographical details. The song reflects one of the hallmarks of chanson: inherent misogyny. Most chanson artists were men, and they often depicted women solely in relation to men (e.g., wives, mothers, lovers, or sex workers) rather than as characters in their own right. "Ne me quitte pas" is no exception since we never hear the voice of the love interest. Scholars of Brel contend that he could "only ever be disappointed in women, since he expect[ed] them to compensate for the failings of his own masculinity."[23] One could argue Brel overperformed self-degrading loss to show what must never actually happen, thus deconstructing masculinity. However, this approach is still rooted in misogyny: "This fear of the power of female sexuality to encroach on the autonomy of the male is a very common theme in *chanson*, and betrays a deeply-rooted mistrust of the opposite sex which is the counterpart of the extremes of dependency expressed in songs like 'Ne me quitte pas.'"[24] Gendered assumptions about heteronormative relationships contributed to these extremes, leaving little room for nuance.

Whether Brel was speaking about his own life through his music, channeling the genre's zeitgeist, or doing a combination of the two, it's up to the audience to question the reliability of both the author and the narrator. While it is generally accepted in literary analysis that an author and narrator should not be conflated, those who study chanson sometimes take a biographical approach that "tends to assume that the real author (Brassens or Brel) and the implied author (the various narrative voices within their songs) are one and the same."[25] Much of the critical analysis of Brel's work has approached his songs as if they are poems to be analyzed and mined for biographical data.[26] For instance, Bruno Hongre and Paul Lidsky study the meaning of Brel's songs through a series of "masks" to help identify the notion of the *héros brélien* (Brelian hero), with the implication that the characters Brel portrays in his songs reveal his fears and, ultimately, who he is.[27]

Writing his own songs strengthened Brel's connection to his characters because it's impossible to completely untangle text and music from a lifetime of experiences. Even though Brel had an acting background and was adept at playing roles, performing his own words allowed him to both act the part of a character and present his true self. By channeling real emotions through his craft, he made his performances more convincing. The audience's desire to connect with the material, in turn, sealed the deal: "Precisely because the narrator sits before us as a human being—albeit a fictionalized one—we naturally react to him in varying degrees in human terms and not just as a disembodied voice providing us with information."[28] This is true of Brel in particular, and singers in general, who live in the public eye. It's hard for an audience to separate the character from the performer when the mental image we've created of the person is similar to the character they're portraying.

Experiencing the Text
The Lyrics

> *Laiss'-moi devenir*
> *L'ombre de ton ombre*
> *L'ombre de ta main*
> *L'ombre de ton chien*

Armed with a French dictionary (this was in the early 2000s, before widespread internet access), I translated "Ne me quitte pas" word for word in an undergraduate French class. The resulting amalgamation of gibberish left me only a little closer to the song's secrets than when I first heard Nina Simone's cover as a teenager. I would need my instructor's help, more French language study, and training in literary analysis to chip away at all its layers.

"Ne me quitte pas" is a lyrical tour de force. It's one of Brel's most literary, poetic, and intimate songs, from the allusions (e.g., the tragic narrator of Stendhal's novel *Le rouge et le noir* [The red and the black], the shadow of unrequited love in Robert Desnos's poem "Le dernier poème," the image of Fyodor Dostoevsky's dog) to the lyrical metaphors of impossibility that form the song's backbone.[29] Nature imagery is particularly evocative in the song—pearls of rain in countries where rain doesn't exist, the spurting volcano believed to be too old. This reliance on nature hints at a perceived "natural" instinct for humans to love.

While the writing in each line is precise, powerful, and imaginative, the structure of the lyrics buttresses the emotions conveyed through words. In some ways the structure is rigid, giving it a sense of finality and immutability. The song is a waltz written in 3/4 time where most syllables in each five-syllable line are an eighth note long.[30] The quarter note at the end of each line emphasizes the meaning of those words, such as the negative marker "pas," which punctuates the narrator's lack of hope. The rhyme scheme also follows a rigid pattern in the first three verses with enclosed rhyme (ABBA). Enclosed rhymes, while somewhat predictable in many types of music, convey a sense of reflection by harking back to the first line in the fourth.

The fourth verse is where "Ne me quitte pas" starts deviating from the ABBA pattern. The unexpected alternating rhyme (ABAB) of the first four lines works to destabilize the listener. The last four rhyming lines ease us into the refrain, whose four-time repetition of the title feels powerful because of the contrast with the enclosed rhyme. Verse 5 continues the upheaval by ending with four lines that have no rhyme at all. This loss of rhyming rigidity builds tension, highlighting the increasing self-deprecation and loss of control the narrator feels, which culminates in his request to become the shadow of his lover's dog.

The song's verb tenses and moods coupled with the descriptive imagery offer yet another way to tap into emotion. The first verse toggles between the past indicative, which nicely reflects the depiction of time (e.g., *temps* [time], *heures* [hours]), forgetfulness (e.g., *oublier* [to forget], *perdu* [lost]), and the imperative, a command that sets the pleading tone of the song. The second and third verses primarily employ the future tense, suggesting the narrator's hope for a different path as he describes his fantastical offerings to placate his lover. The third verse is temporally complex in how the narrator reverts to the past tense in telling the story of the king who dies from lost love. This mixing of storytelling with future personal desires allows for a mingling of multiple characters and time scales. Furthermore, the lyrics mirror this blending of perspectives when the narrator indicates it's his lover the king cannot find. There is a sense that losing love isn't a singular phenomenon endured by an individual but a fate many others have experienced. The fourth verse uses present, past, and future tense to make the impossible possible with the image of growth springing from devastation and death—a signal the narrator hasn't quite given up: "Il est, paraît-il, des terres brûlées donnant plus de blé qu'un meilleur avril" (It seems that scorched earth is yielding more wheat than the best April).[31] The fifth verse contains the only *futur proche* of the whole song (i.e., "Je n'vais plus pleurer. Je n'vais plus parler" [I'm no longer going to cry. I'm no longer going to speak]). The *futur proche* in French conveys an immediacy that the *futur simple* (e.g., "Je me cach'rai là" [I'll hide there]) does not. At the same time, the *futur proche* can act as a command. In this case, the narrator wills himself not to cry or speak anymore. Then the narrator employs the imperative mood ("Laiss'-moi devenir l'ombre de ton ombre" [Let me become the shadow of your shadow])—another command and final plea for what has proven a lost cause.

The Music

While the lyrics channel desperation and self-pity, the musical aspects work with the words to further enhance these emotions and our response to them.[32] The music was always my first entrée into the world of this song. Similar to how the longer notes at the end of each line add rhythmic emphasis to those syllables, the change in pitch in the middle of each line creates a melodic shape that swells at the center of each thought. I find myself humming the melody long after I've listened to the song because of the poignancy evoked by the vacillation between the chord tone and neighboring tone. The melodic idea employs exact repetition for a few bars before the starting note descends the scale. This falling melody conjures sadness, as if the narrator marches toward despair, but then quickly ascends after the refrain, providing contrast and a surge of hope.

Furthermore, just as he expands the metaphorical world of the song through literary allusions, Brel seemingly borrows classical musical themes, such as hints of the second movement of Franz

Liszt's Hungarian Rhapsody no. 6.[33] Meanwhile, Peter Hawkins demonstrates how the song "bears a considerable resemblance to 'Le Roi a fait battre tambour': it is as if Brel was unconsciously improvising variations on its underlying theme of tragic, unrequited love in the elaboration of his own song."[34] This baroque French folk song, which Édith Piaf and many others have sung, occupies an important place in the French cultural imaginary and speaks to a long-standing French musical tradition. As such, Brel taps into a certain ethos that contemporary French audiences are accustomed to and can connect with.

"Ne me quitte pas" also exudes harmonic richness. Hawkins lauds Brel's "technical skill as songwriter, devising memorable melodies and refrains which combine poetic suggestiveness with immediate comprehensibility, through the clever deployment of repetition and variation."[35] The repeating title line in the refrain is probably the most striking use of repetition and contrast. The repetition of both lyrics and the melodic idea suggests desperate pleading that is convincing on its own merits, but the changing harmony further highlights overwhelming emotions. A different chord buttresses each "ne me quitte pas," which recontextualizes the melody by changing the relationship between the note and the chord. While the lyrical and melodic repetition connotes incessant begging, the contrasting harmony conveys the building intensity of surging and complex feelings. The dominant and seventh chords throughout the song, but especially in the refrain, provide an additional emotional punch by adding tension.

The different cadences of the lines contribute to the sense of being on an emotional rollercoaster. Most lines in the verses go from the V to the Im chord. This full cadence offers resolution to the listener, strengthening the underlying emotions of loss and hopelessness that the narrator conveys. However, the refrain uses the half cadence ending on V, which injects a sense of longing through the lack of resolution. Perhaps things will be OK. This contrast between the refrain and verse further highlights the narrator's anxiety and despair embodied with each "ne me quitte pas."

Repetition and variation also mark the verses. The same chords repeat throughout most of the song, usually some variation of Im, Im^7, IVm, and V^7, with each chord taking up a full bar. However, the harmonic rhythm accelerates during the most poignant sections of the song, such as when the narrator promises to achieve impossible feats. Furthermore, the occasional surprising chord highlights the significance of certain words and phrases. For instance, in Brel's 1966 performance, he seems to tonicize the relative C major on the word *lumière* by using a B-natural leading note, creating a brief, happy atmosphere and setting up a major clash with the G minor from outside the key when the narrator describes love as king.[36] The B-flat in the melody has a strong downward pull, which firmly modulates the harmony back to the relative minor and its somber tone. Happiness is nothing but a fleeting illusion. Each harmonic decision Brel utilizes in his writing or performing transforms a relatively simple melody into an emotionally charged dirge of a man mourning the death of love.

Jean-François Kahn's obituary beautifully sums up the power of Brel's writing: "Brel était un authentique poète et...il savait chanter avec des mots ce qu'il pouvait écrire avec des notes. Chez lui, la mélodie n'était pas seulement le réceptacle du message, mais sa sève" (Brel was a genuine poet who knew how to sing with words what he could write with notes. With him the melody is not merely the vehicle of a message, but its lifeblood).[37] I would argue, however, that it's Brel's attention to harmony that really gives this song life.

The Performance

While emotion runs through the lyrics and composition, the way Brel performed "Ne me quitte pas" takes the song to new heights. My favorite version is from what was billed as his last televised performance.

After years of exhausting concert schedules and personal set-backs, including the loss of both parents, Brel announced his retirement from touring in late 1966. In October he embarked on a farewell tour, which included several concerts at Paris's famed Olympia music hall. In November, *Palmarès des chansons* (The chart show), a weekly variety show that aired in prime time on Channel 1 between 1965 and 1968, invited Brel to commemorate his farewell to the stage. Celebrities from the entertainment world filled the Maison de la Radio in the sixteenth arrondissement, a grateful audience paying tribute to a legend.

The episode begins with an interview of Brel, followed by various musician friends, such as Juliette Greco, Jean Poiret, and Pia Colombo, singing some of his hits. Brel, backed by his orchestra, then performs about a dozen songs. "Ne me quitte pas," coming in the middle of this retrospective, stands out visually. While the preceding and following songs are filmed with alternating long and medium shots, "Ne me quitte pas" is filmed in close-up from start to finish. For someone like me watching the archival recording decades later, this framing choice has a profound effect—I can focus so closely on Brel's face that I feel as if I'm there.

Much has been said about Brel's physicality and how well he embodied the figure of the chansonnier. Preperformance vomiting and sweat-drenched microphones "contribute to the image of the singer-songwriter strenuously working to deliver the best of himself to his audience."[38] However, looking past the more demonstrative aspects of his stage presence uncovers Brel's success at conveying subtlety. This performance starts with Brel staring downward as he enunciates the title line. By the time he gets to *oublier* (forget) in the next line, he has lifted his eyes to meet our gaze. He then blinks in rapid succession for a couple of lines, which gives off a sense of anxiety. He spends the next few lines barely blinking at all before closing his eyes conspicuously on the word *pourquoi* (why). At that moment, the timbre in his voice becomes very raspy, adding to the gravitas his heavy eyelids portray. When he arrives at the refrain, he shakes his head vigorously for each "ne me quitte pas," as if overcome with nervous energy. At the same time, his volume lowers to a whisper until the last *pas,* a marker of negation, which is articulated but silent.

The next verse begins with a loud, drawn-out *moi* (me), which calls attention to the narrator not only through the word itself but also through how it is uttered. The whole verse is at an elevated volume, suggesting determination as the narrator enumerates the things he will give to his lover to make her stay. Brel also locks eyes with his viewer, conveying resolve to follow through on these impossible promises. He then looks up to the heavens in an almost spiritual pose when he talks about love being king and law. After this he returns to the refrain, singing it more forcefully than the last time but also inserting pregnant pauses, particularly before the last *pas*, for dramatic effect.

Brel's use of rubato, where he stretches certain phrases and moves quickly through others, enhances the musical construction of the song and its rhythmic intensity. He sings the verses that have a higher register (verses 2 and 4) more quickly and follows them with a short piano interlude. Because the music does not stop at the end of the line, there is an overflowing kind of vibe that enhances the emotional intensity. The way the speed alternates from verse to verse creates a structure that infuses more drama than there would otherwise be. There are also many instances where he pauses unexpectedly before running lines together, such as between the fourth verse and the refrain. This temporal elasticity acts like a yo-yo that discombobulates the listener. It's understandable why Brel has been depicted as a miracle worker in his ability to "suspend time, warp time, shape time, until it is tickless, seamless"—a trait that stands out in "Ne me quitte pas."[39]

Knowing Brel assumed this would be his last televised concert puts such time dilation in further relief because this moment has the atemporality of historical significance. Meanwhile, the narrator's entreaties to an unnamed interlocuter could be read as a performer begging his audience not to abandon him as he leaves the public eye at the height of his career. The cultural importance of the performance blurs the line between narrator, audience, and artist even more.

Affect, Authenticity, and Emotional Truthfulness

Each time I watch Brel sing this song and experience the pain of abandonment through his eyes, I fall into the trap of wondering who the song is for and to what extent it chronicles real life. For what it's worth, Brel has convinced me of the song's truth, despite dismissing autobiographical readings. For instance, the changes in volume, facial expressions, timbre, and tempo that are integral to his performance serve to highlight the presentation of a "real" voice for most of the song. As L. J. Müller argues, a real voice is "a style of singing connected to aesthetic paradigms of emotional truthfulness, spontaneity and authenticity" and "contains an invitation to identification, which further fosters the privileging of a hegemonic White male concept of the body."[40] I interpret Brel's attempt to perform masculinity by fighting for (and failing to win) a lost love as a sort of tragic heroism.[41] His mentor Édith Piaf, however, hated the song, arguing that a man should maintain his dignity and never stoop so low. Brel's convincing performance thus transgresses appropriate and accepted expressions of masculinity.[42]

Brel's use of vibrato, cracking voice, audible breathing, unstable timing, and unexpected pauses suggest genuineness conveyed through an apparent loss of control.[43] The narrator seems to be fighting his own subconsciousness, which doesn't want to accept loss. The first refrain's unheard *pas* can be seen as an inner withdrawal, which is then countered by the emphasized *moi* and energetic vocalization in the second verse, as if the narrator must remind himself to fight. Meanwhile, the structural aspects, such as the breakdown of the rhyme scheme, support the performative expression of failure and unraveling control. The contrast between outward-directed fight and inward-directed sadness is relatable and thus feels real. Being a chansonnier is all about authenticity, and Brel's success as a lyricist, composer, and performer brands him as one of the most authentic chanson artists there is.[44]

These different aspects of his performance convince many listeners of his realness, but part of what we tap into are the emotions he expresses. When I listen to "Ne me quitte pas," I don't just ponder it in my mind. I feel and experience it deeply within my body.[45] In a way, my body orients itself toward the song's emotion. In her theorization of affect and emotion, Sara Ahmed describes how "emotions are directed to what we come into contact with: they move us 'toward' and 'away' from such objects."[46] It's through this emotional tether that a song and listener move in relation to each other.

In an analysis of this performance, one of my students remarked that she could see the cowardice in his eyes and felt them pulling her in. She felt compelled to move closer to the screen, literally. Listeners orient themselves toward music and experience emotion as an embodied act in which emotions are temporally located and manifest on the body: "For an object to make this impression is dependent on past histories, which surface as impressions on the skin. At the same time, emotions shape what bodies do in the present, or how they are moved by the objects they approach."[47] My memories of—and present-day bodily reactions to—"Ne me quitte pas" convey the stakes of becoming involved with a song. The oscillation between past and present indicates the temporal journey of music as it connects us to the past, present, and future.

While a psychological perspective conceives of emotion as something we experience inside ourselves, Ahmed takes a primarily sociological and anthropological approach to affect that views emotions as social and cultural practices.[48] Considering both the psychological and sociocultural, I'm most interested in how texts/performances produce sonic and embodied tensions and how these emotions travel on a song. Advances in technology allowed Brel's performance to extend far past the performance he gave his studio audience. That night, Brel's performance reached nearly twenty million French homes. Filmed live on kinescope (a 16mm film camera pointed at a TV screen), it was also recorded for posterity.[49] Now a part of INA's repository of French audiovisual media and available online to the public since the mid-2000s, this performance of "Ne me quitte pas" is preserved as part of French cultural heritage. INA's official YouTube channel, launched a few years later, made Brel even more accessible globally.[50] Hundreds of comments and 1.6 million views later, viewers still share their emotional journeys and reminisce about hearing him sing for the first time. Whether one was in the audience, watching the live transmission at home, or viewing the recording on YouTube decades later, the interaction of lyrics, music, and performance impart the ability to experience emotion and to connect with others within a nation-state (e.g., France or Belgium), a region (e.g., the francophone world), or across the world.

Concluding Thoughts

Each time I listen to my French students discuss their emotional experiences with "Ne me quitte pas," I'm catapulted back to my undergraduate days with Brel and my high school days with Simone. I wonder where this song will lead these French majors. Will it have the same effect on their lives as it has had on mine? Will they one day ride the notes of a song to get to where they want to go?

I have expanded on Loisy's metaphor about Brel being a journey and situated "Ne me quitte pas" within Brel's life and the genre of chanson, demonstrating the different paths a song can take. Blurring the line between artistic creativity and autobiography, chanson brings culturally relevant experiences to the stage as a sort of travel through storytelling. Brel also crosses borders by using both art and language to transcend nationality—the Belgian exemplar of French exceptionalism. Furthermore, his embodiment of a persona through his convincing performances is a form of travel from a person to a character. Regardless of the extent to which a song is based on real life, as listeners we engage with the emotions all the same. As such, Ahmed's conceptualization of how emotions move us in relation to objects demonstrates how a song is a vehicle through which emotions travel. Brel is exceptional in his ability to marry language, music, and performance in a way that allows intense emotions to be conveyed through song and felt by listeners. The blurring of reality and art means that it's especially important to analyze who is seen as real and who has access to constructions of realness in popular music.

▶ 02 "Sorry about the Words, Y'all"

Nina Simone Covers Brel

ON JUNE 10, 1988, Thierry Ardisson interviewed Nina Simone at Les Bains Douches nightclub in Paris for his weekly late-night show *Bains de minuit* (Midnight baths) on the TV network La Cinq.[1] In this episode, Simone sits behind a circular table large enough for only two people. Positioned in the center of the frame and exuding her indomitable presence, she faces the camera with her gold eyeshadow subtly shimmering. The viewer sees Ardisson only in profile. Bathed in a dim, blue light, they sip champagne, smoke cigarettes, and chat in English. I strain to hear the original English because the French dubbing overpowers Simone's thoughtful response to Ardisson about why she chose to sing "Ne me quitte pas," one of her only French-language songs. Simone recounts how a friend in New York played a recording of the song—Brel's iconic single—insisting she incorporate it into her repertoire because he knew she could do it well. Remembering that first listening experience, she remarks, "At that time, I did not know what these words meant. . . . I didn't know what the man said, but when he said, 'Ne me quitte pas,' I started crying. And I said I know that's a very sad song."

As Simone shared her overwhelming emotional response to Brel's plaintive melody, I thought about how she would have that same effect on generations to come. Thirty years after that interview, Mary J. Blige related a similar experience during her speech at Simone's induction into the Rock and Roll Hall of Fame: "When I heard 'Ne me quitte pas' for the first time, the song she sang in French, I couldn't understand a word she was saying. . . . But I felt everything she was saying, all this deep emotion and pain of her longing for someone seems to be what she was singing about."[2] This time it was Simone's single that wielded the power. Thinking about my own relationship to "Ne me quitte pas," I marvel at the various iterations of this first encounter and how the retellings travel through time and space.

Covering, Musical Marronage, and a Parisian Legacy

I vividly remember the consternation on a high school class-mate's face when I blasphemously confessed that I usually pre-fer covers of Beatles' songs to the originals. I couldn't help it—I respected the Beatles for their songwriting genius, but Boyz II Men's and En Vogue's "Yesterday" and Stevie Wonder's "We Can Work It Out" spoke to me in ways the originals never did.

My friend's points—about the value of originals, about the Beatles being the greatest band ever—couldn't overcome my deep-seated connection to various Beatles' covers. Our debate became a full-fledged argument when I threw down that Ike and Tina Turner's "Proud Mary" left CCR's version in the dust. While I believed what I was saying, there was also a racial sub-text: being the only Black girl in my senior class inspired me to uplift Black excellence any chance I got. It wasn't until I watched Lisa Cortés's documentary *Little Richard: I Am Everything* that I became acutely aware of the racial implications of my feelings.

Covering—the performing or recording of a song by an artist who isn't credited with the original release or performance of it—is a mainstream concept.[3] Cover songs didn't exist until the invention of recorded songs, which created authoritative per-formances against which a cover could be measured. Sound recording allowed a song to be identified in an original form and defined by its iterability and capacity for circulation in different contexts—the birth of the single.[4] However, Pat Boone's lackluster cover of "Tutti Frutti" outsold Little Richard's, and Elvis Presley's cover of "Hound Dog" rocketed him to stardom, while Big Mama Thornton's original only found success on the R&B charts and didn't translate into a prosperous career. These examples demonstrate that there are restrictions on how Black music can circulate as well as the claims Black musicians can make on certain musical genres.[5]

There is a long history of Black erasure in popular music. In his deep dive into "Hound Dog" Eric Weisbard writes, "Black music, especially as performed by Black women, was buried by white rock's self-serving mythology and now sorely needs reclamation."[6] Instead of engaging in this important work of restoring Black musicians to their rightful place as originators, my reclamation takes on a different but complementary focus. I explore how a Black American, English-speaking woman could, against all odds, successfully make a claim on a white Belgian man's French-language song. The words of Zandria Robinson guide me in this effort; when reflecting on the Black musicians who inspired Little Richard, she remarks, "It is [a] case of witness. They are . . . the mirrors that come into your life to show you who you really are."[7] In some ways, covering is a case of witness. "Ne me quitte pas" helped Simone figure out who she was, and in return she helped the song travel in ways the original did not.

According to the website Brelitude.net, which maintains an impressive list of Jacques Brel covers, his music has been covered more than nine thousand times.[8] "Ne me quitte pas" tops the list with 1,683 entries.[9] Of these covers, Simone's version is the one that elicits the strongest emotional response from me, both for the ways she performs it and for how I relate to her as a Black American woman singing in a foreign language. When Simone covered it on her 1965 album *I Put a Spell on You*, it was one of three French-language songs she included. The others were "L'amour, c'est comme un jour" ("Tomorrow Is My Turn") and "Il faut savoir" ("You've Got to Learn"), both by the Armenian French chanson artist Charles Aznavour, for which Simone bought the rights in 1962.[10] The inclusion of these three songs indicates Simone's reverence for the chanson genre. It's striking, however, that of the three, Simone chose to sing only "Ne me quitte pas" in the original French.[11] One imagines that if Simone really wanted to sing the song in English she could easily have found a translator, especially since Rod McKuen's "If You Go Away" came out a year later. Regardless of whether Simone's decision to record "Ne me quitte pas" in French was primarily logistical or artistic, the impact remains the same: her cover has had a profound effect on francophone and anglophone audiences throughout the world, and her use of French has allowed the language to travel in ways that wouldn't have been possible if she had sung in English.

When Simone covered songs, especially this one, she both embodied the original and added flourishes to make it her own.[12] Her musical stylings and orchestration have been described as "effective because Nina sang with such conviction," such as with

"Jacques Brel's 'Ne me quitte pas,' a song that pleads, 'don't leave me.' Surrounded by strings again, Nina cast herself as a chanteuse."[13] Simone's French stage name and convincing chanteuse persona so personified the essence of chanson that "some initially assumed that she was a 'French chanteuse.'"[14] Others have suggested Simone is the only person whose interpretation of "Ne me quitte pas" rivals that of Brel's.[15] Her version is so important to the francophone world that when Presses de la Renaissance published the French translation of *I Put a Spell on You: The Autobiography of Nina Simone* in 1991, the publisher retitled it *Ne me quittez pas: Mémoires.*[16]

What was it about Simone that allowed listeners to imagine her as a chanson singer when her repertoire included so few chanson songs? For one, she started her career in supper clubs, which were similar to the French music halls known for chanson. Her decision to sing Kurt Weill and Bertolt Brecht's "Pirate Jenny" harked back to her connection to this supper club genre. In fact, Daphne Brooks has labeled Simone "the most prominent African American interpreter" of Weill and Brecht's work, lauding her ability to recontextualize their Weimer Republic theatrics in the era of the American civil rights movement.[17] Performing "Ne me quitte pas" in French was just another example of Simone taking a song that seemed distant from her usual material and convincingly making it her own.

Simone was effective in achieving what Brooks has conceptualized as musical marronage, an ability to escape the confines of genres and audience expectations of singers. As the choice of the word suggests—maroonage means to free oneself from enslavement—Brooks centers Simone's Blackness and the restrictions Black singers, especially Black women, encounter: "She forged her own form of musical integration and performative agitation, crossing the lines of musical genres . . . and defamiliarizing cultural expectations of where black women can and should articulate their voices and musicianship aesthetically and politically."[18] So while critics may pin Simone to a certain genre—was she a jazz artist, a blues artist, a classical artist, a pop artist, all or none of the above?—I appreciate Brooks's reframing of the question to ask, "What should a black female artist sound like?"[19] As someone who has spent my life fielding questions about my voice (Is it Black enough? French enough? Scholarly enough? Real enough?), I often reflect on my own sonic journey. Brooks homes in on what first drew me to Simone. Her songs serve "as sonic struggles in and of themselves, as embattled efforts to elude generic categorizations as a black female performer."[20] As Simone admitted, "It's always been my aim to stay outside any category. . . . That's my freedom."[21] Brooks offers an important model in understanding what Simone accomplished through her musical maroonage—a useful tool that can be applied to Simone's contributions to both American music and French and francophone culture.

In discussing Simone's covering and musical maroonage, it's important to understand the context in which she performed "Ne me quitte pas." There was already a long tradition of African American creatives in France when Simone arrived on the French scene.[22] In the eighteenth and especially the nineteenth centuries, wealthy Creoles of color from Louisiana like Victor Séjour, author of *The Mulatto* (the earliest known work of African American fiction, published in French in 1837), often studied in Paris. Later, World War I brought a new influx of Black Americans to France, including the forty to fifty thousand troops serving under French commanders (e.g., the 369th "Harlem Hell Fighters" Infantry Regiment). Many stayed after the war to avoid the segregation and inhumane treatment that awaited them back home. They found Paris accepting of Black Americans who offered something in return. In particular, Paris was hungry for Black entertainers. For instance, African American military pilot Eugene Bullard reinvented himself as a jazz drummer even though he had never before played the instrument. Parisians at the time believed only Black musicians could play jazz authentically, and many Black Americans thrived by exploiting this prejudice.

Paris in the 1920s witnessed a renaissance for Black American performers (e.g., Josephine Baker, Ada Louise "Bricktop" Smith, Florence Jones), writers (e.g., Langston Hughes, Claude McKay, Gwendolyn Bennett), and artists (e.g., Anna Julia Cooper, Henry Ossawa Tanner), all of whom flocked to the city to receive respect for their craft and opportunities not afforded them in the United States. By the 1960s, when Simone arrived, Paris had lost some of its allure as a color-blind mecca, with such authors as

James Baldwin and William Gardner Smith chronicling the complex racialized experiences of Black Americans and other members of the African diaspora. However, as we will see in Simone's own words, France still offered less of a racial sting than what she encountered in the United States. It also allowed Simone to break free of constraints she fought against back home. I suspect that "Ne me quitte pas" was the most productive for musical maroonage out of her vast catalog because of the doors that singing in French opened for her. At the same time, she took "Ne me quitte pas" to new heights.

Experiencing the Text

> *Moi, je t'offrirai*
> *Des perles de pluie*
> *Venues de pays*
> *Où il ne pleut pas*

In many ways, Simone's studio version of "Ne me quitte pas" adheres closely to Brel's.[23] While some of her contemporaries made changes to reflect a female perspective, Simone is notable for her fidelity to the lyrics. Simone Langlois, who recorded this song in 1959, around the same time as Brel, modifies "où l'amour s'ra roi" (where love'll be king) to "où tu seras roi" (where you will be king) before feminizing the narrator to make her queen ("où je serai reine" instead of "où je serai roi").[24] In her 1963 version, Barbara also substitutes the line "où je serai reine" (I will be queen).[25] She then avoids the line "l'ombre de ton chien" (the shadow of your dog), opting instead for "je ne dirai plus rien" (I will say no more), which suggests she takes issue with the idea of debasing oneself to be less than even a dog's shadow. Interestingly, Langlois performs this line but seems to lack conviction when compared to Simone and Brel, who both sing it with vocal strain, as if pain rides each note. As such, Simone does more than simply preserve the original lyrics. By using her vocal performance to convincingly express meaning, she preserves the emotions Brel meticulously crafted. The timbre of her voice is perfect for a song that drips with despair.

Simone may not modify the gender because she is a non-native French speaker and feels somewhat removed from the lyrics' grammatical implications. However, her singing to a female interlocutor could also be a nod to her alleged bisexuality. Simone never came out as bisexual but indicated having at least one sexual relationship with a woman, whom Simone deeply loved.[26] In keeping Brel's lyrics intact, she influences how listeners understand the song and imagine its possibilities. Sometimes doing nothing yields the greatest effect.

While the 1965 recording is a solid cover, her live performances of "Ne me quitte pas" are what distinguish her from Brel. They also underscore her sonic struggles and the freedom she achieves through musical marronage. In her December 18, 1971, performance (recorded in front of a live audience and broadcast on state-run Channel 2), Simone draws her magic from the piano keys, highlighting what's missing in the studio recording, which relies heavily on string accompaniment.[27] In my opinion, Simone always seems most comfortable when she loses herself in the piano, and this comfort is on full display here. For instance, after the refrain she inserts captivating interludes full of arpeggios and hard-struck chords. She moves up the piano and then back down, interspersing pregnant pauses when lingering on certain notes. Her face remains calm throughout, as if in a meditative state. The interludes allow Simone to show off the full range of her artistic skills without the constraints of a disappointing accompaniment. In particular, the triangle and percussion's timing seem off, forcing her to constantly grate against an inadequate structure that fails to support her through the song.

The piano's powerful presence is put in further relief when she suppresses it to sing the tonic pronoun *moi*, followed by a long, almost uncomfortable pause in the line "moi, je t'offrirai" (I will offer you). Eliminating the piano heightens this word, which is grammatically unnecessary but emphasizes the first-person subject *je* and underlines the importance of the narrator. This unsupported note also conveys incredible vulnerability and a sense of being exposed that allows the listener to deeply feel the narrator's despair.[28]

In addition to the piano's effect, Simone shifts the temporal flow of each line by elongating some words and shortening others. She spends an inordinately long time on *coups*, *coeur*, and *bonheur* in "à coups de pourquoi le coeur du bonheur" (repeatedly asking the heart of happiness why). In other places, time ebbs and flows in unexpected ways because of where she speeds up and pauses. For instance, when she sings, "Oublier le temps des malentendus et [*pause*] le temps perdu à savoir comment" (forget the time of misunderstandings and [*pause*] the time lost trying to know how), she quickly passes between lines but pauses within a line. Through pauses, run-ons, and tempo changes throughout the song, Simone plays with time, but differently than Brel does. Because it defies expectations, her approach is more unsettling. In both cases, the time dilation imbues the lyrics with extra meaning. Just as a bad breakup can distort a lover's sense of time, making good memories pass quickly and the pain of rejection seem endless, Simone evokes the fickleness of time and its relationship to our perception of reality.[29]

Simone also astutely modulates her volume and vocal timbre. She almost whispers in the first refrain before gradually increasing volume in the second verse until her microphone appears to clip the word *lumière* (light). The clipping is yet another indication that the structure (this time of sound engineering instead of musical accompaniment) stifles her performance. However, the subpar audio doesn't dampen the emotion Simone conjures through her intentional use of volume. In fact, the inadequate structure serves to remind us how adept she is at breaking free.

When Simone sings, "Des perles de pluie" (pearls of rain), the timbre in her voice takes a raspy quality. Then, when she enunciates, "Je t'inventerai" (I will invent for you), she sings breathily and tapers at the end, conveying exacerbation. A couple lines later, she almost speaks instead of sings the word *comprendras* (you will understand). Her singing voice morphs into speech again with the line "je te parlerai de ces amants-là" (I will tell you of those lovers), which sounds more like a narration of a fairy tale than the singing of a ballad. In addition, the way her gaze moves to the audience with "je te parlerai" is quite arresting. Meanwhile, in the fourth verse she takes her hands off the piano for the word *vu* (seen), raises them to head level, and pauses before singing the word *souvent* (often). Here her voice almost cracks under its own desperation.[30]

However, the most effective use of timbre occurs when Simone sings the refrain for the second time, articulating the lyrics' desperation through multiple strategies. When she first says, "Ne me quitte pas," it almost sounds as if she's crying; you can hear the wetness in her voice. Then she inserts a drawn-out "Oh," followed by a pause then a strained "Oh Lord" that bleeds into "Ne me quitte pas," sung four times quickly, with each iteration quieter and thinner than the last, like a cascading waterfall losing intensity. She inserts English again in the fourth refrain, saying, "Sorry about the words, y'all," after the first "ne me quitte pas." She then repeats the title phrase three more times before ending the song without singing the final verse.

Breaking Free: Language, Race, and the Quest for Realness

The English in Simone's version is jarring. Although its usage is minimal, the effects are massive because of what it can tell us about the experiences of Simone and her audiences. While her pronunciation in this live performance approaches that of a native French speaker more closely than her studio version from six years prior, there are moments where she hesitates (e.g., the *l* in *loi*, the *r* in *noir*). By 1971 Simone had spent quite a bit of time in francophone countries and practiced and performed the song many times. However, her apology and her cutting the song short suggest that the French language is at the forefront of her mind—a recognition of possible linguistic hostility.

In fact, in her interview with Ardisson, she reenacted her difficulties with "Ne me quitte pas": "I couldn't pronounce the word *creuserai*, and I couldn't pronounce the word R-O-I and L-O-I. And for two years in Switzerland, when I was studying that song, I had to make exceptions for those two words R-O-I, which means 'king,' right, and L-O-I, which means 'law.'"[31] Simone worked with a professor who had her repeat the lyrics phonetically for years before she dared sing the song in public.[32]

While I haven't found contemporary music critiques focusing on the song's language, recent YouTube comments from francophone speakers point to the central concern of language in Simone's covers of "Ne me quitte pas." Of the studio recording,

@cyrilfrnt, who identifies as French, writes, "I love Nina Simone, but this version doesn't convey any emotion, she's just struggling to pronounce words and they barely mean anything. I guess non-French speaking people can still like it, but for us it's not enjoyable."[33] They express their admiration of Simone as an artist and generally like her work, so their critique of her is specifically about "Ne me quitte pas." Perhaps Simone was accustomed to this type of commentary, given her midsong apology about the words in the 1971 live recording. @stanleywlodyka3663 picks up on Simone's preoccupation with the following comment on this live version: "She seems frustrated in this performance. I thought it was interesting that she was singing a French song to a French audience. She must have been aware that she would be scrutinized not only for her pronunciation but also because she chose to do such a famous French song."[34] While I don't read frustration here (an emotion Simone was known to express when she thought an audience wasn't giving her the respect she deserved), this comment captures the weight of the lyrics on Simone and the expectations of the audience.[35]

The commentors' preoccupation with Simone's French pronunciation is indicative of a much larger phenomenon in France and, to a lesser extent, other francophone countries. Discussions of correct usage of French is practically a national pastime in France, where "the standard language is viewed in the French tradition as a *trésor* [treasure], a *patrimoine* [heritage]—an institution, which has been elaborated and perfected over time."[36]

France's national identity is inextricably linked not just to the French language, but to standard French marked by a supposed neutral accent.[37] Nonstandard usage in pronunciation, grammar, and other linguistic factors is disparaged. Even though Brel was Belgian, he moved to France in his early twenties. In one interview, he discussed picking up the *accent pointu* often associated with Parisians.[38] More important, Brel's mastery of literary and poetic French made him an ambassador of the French language. Furthermore, as a white European man, he embodied the normative image of a French speaker. Simone, who didn't speak French at the time of the studio recording and was still learning by the time of the live performance, transgressed linguistic and racial expectations associated with French, especially considering language's importance in chanson music.

There is no doubt Simone spoke French as a nonnative speaker, with the pronunciation and grammar usage expected from a learner of French.[39] However, even if the comments are true, conceptualizations of race still play a role. In my time living in Paris, I witnessed native French speakers ridiculed for speaking French while Black: "Linguistic competence was often determined by more than just one's ability to use a language well; one's linguistic competence depended on the ability to prove cultural legitimacy, which extended beyond language to include other identity markers, most notably race."[40] Furthermore, in the context of popular music, it seems acceptable to appropriate African languages without care for pronunciation or meaning (e.g.,

"Waka Waka," "The Lion Sleeps Tonight"). However, someone like Simone is criticized despite all her effort and care in learning the lyrics, which suggests power differentials in global cultural discourses. In response to @cyrilfrnt, commenter @Rosannasfriend conveys their exacerbation when defending Simone: "Who cares if she cannot pronounce the words properly? She tried. French people pronounce English badly all the time and English people allow them to get away with it and don't make them feel like they can't speak the language or practice it with us."[41] While this comment doesn't focus on race, it hints at a much larger global context around language and belonging and the double standards that require perfection from minoritized individuals.

The racial subtext in seemingly race-neutral commentary is even more prevalent when discussing Simone as a musician. A review in the *Jacksonville Free Press* highlights Simone's impressive range: "It is her innate skill at putting her own distinctive stamp on such a diverse range of material that has made Nina Simone a legend in her own time: she finds the perfect interpretation for each song she selects."[42] Innateness is a descriptor that could be used for any musician, but the abilities of Black artists—especially in genres that rely heavily on improvisation—are often described as "innate" or "natural," which effaces the labor, creativity, and artistry that make an artist great.[43] After all, this assumption of innateness was why 1920s Paris opened its doors to Black jazz musicians. For her part, Simone credited her success both to her natural abilities and her strong work ethic.[44]

Equally important, Simone called out critics' lack of imagination when they labeled her with Black-coded language: "I didn't like to be put in a box with other jazz singers because my musicianship was totally different, and in its own way superior. Calling me a jazz singer was a way of ignoring my musical background because I didn't fit into white ideas of what a black performer should be. It was a racist thing; 'If she's black she must be a jazz singer.'"[45]

While Simone pushed against constraints that equated Blackness with jazz, she also embraced all the facets of her being, including her Blackness, in complex ways. Her use of "Oh Lord" in the second verse introduces a world that is not only linguistically foreign to the song and the genre but also culturally rich, historically relevant, and representative of Simone's lived experiences. In my own listening, the "Oh Lord" gestures to Black spirituals and their role in survival. For instance, Geneva Smitherman details the linguistic agency of enslaved Africans who used coded religious words and imagery to escape their oppressors: "They moaned 'steal away to Jesus' to mean stealing away FROM the plantation TO freedom (That is, 'Jesus')."[46] It would be hard to argue that Simone accomplishes literal maroonage simply by inserting an "Oh Lord" in a French-language breakup song. However, as Mark Anthony Neal argues, there is a transcendence of time and space "through the creation of metaphoric landscapes rooted in literal communal efforts to subvert unacceptable conditions" in what he calls "hostile linguistic and social terrain."[47]

What if the "Oh Lord" does more than capture the perspective of a grieving narrator? What if it gives the listener insight into the performer's mindset and the baggage she carries?

Even though Simone's legacy is marked in complicated ways by her push for civil rights and racial justice, I see the way she existed in the music world as revolutionary, even when she wasn't using her music as protest. As Brooks argues, "Black women's musical practices are, in short, revolutionary because they are inextricably linked to the matter of Black life" and "because of the ways in which said practices both forecast and execute the viability and potentiality of Black life."[48] Singing a song like "Ne me quitte pas," which tells of individual heartbreak instead of societal injustice, offered Simone a respite from the anguish of singing protest music, a genre that implored the world to see her humanity and her right to exist at great emotional cost.[49] It also shielded her from the pain of constantly being reduced to a racialized and gendered Other. Singing in French further removed her from the brutal American context she sought to escape, especially after she was ostracized for her 1964 song "Mississippi Goddam." It's noteworthy that the live recording analyzed here occurred around the time she left the United States because of fallout from her protest music.[50] "Ne me quitte pas" permitted Simone to sing about her life, Black life, without naming race, while the anguished "Oh Lord" reminds the listener that race is never absent from the Black experience. In other words, instead of understanding race as an innate quality that predisposes someone to excel at a certain genre, I see race as a set of lived interactions with the world. Channeling these experiences in music allows a performer to expand genres, complicate conceptualizations of Blackness, and practice musical maroonage.

But what does all this mean for conveying authenticity? As I argued in chapter 1, Brel sings with a real voice because the story of the text matches what his performance depicts, convincing the listener of authentic emotion. Can we say the same for Simone? In not modifying the gender of the narrator in "Ne me quitte pas," is Simone impersonating Brel, a white man, and imagining herself addressing a woman from this imagined position? Is she singing as a woman to a woman, expressing queerness and being authentic in ways she couldn't easily do in real life? Are the lyrics inconsequential, and she is instead performing emotions that go beyond romantic love and loss? Or is she oscillating across multiple perspectives?

Furthermore, what is the audience hearing, and how does reception differ depending on the person? Would a French speaker who understands the lyrics hear the realness of the voice differently than an ardent fan who knows the specificity of Simone's voice? As someone who speaks French and knows Simone's music well, I find that my engagement wavers. More specifically, when I focus on the grammar and the content of the lyrics, I more easily separate Simone from the text's meaning and emotion. At these times, she seems to impersonate a white heterosexual man and the tortured romantic experience he narrates.

But when her voice is my primary concern, I picture her face and reflect on her life and her struggles to be accepted as human. For their class assignment, one of my students wrote that Simone's version touched her heart because Simone sings as if the words are escaping from the depths of her soul. The emotions she conveys seem very real channeling a lifetime of heartache not only from failed romantic relationships but also from failed relationships with a racist American society that would rather she not exist and a music industry that took advantage of her.[51]

Returning to Müller's treatment of voice, one could read Simone as pulling off a very convincing real voice, much like the contemporary British artist Birdy does in her performance of "People Help the People." In commenting on how the listener can identify with Birdy's brittle voice, Müller argues that "the vibrating breathing gives the impression of a lack of control over the vocalization, which can be interpreted as an expression of her sincerely felt grief. The voice appears 'genuine' in that it credibly communicates a present somatic-emotional state."[52] Müller adds that an apparent loss of body control is needed to convey genuine sadness, something Birdy performs well despite a very controlled performance. Similarly, Simone convincingly expresses sadness, despair, and loss through her embodied emotional responses (vibrato, almost-breaking voice, struggle with pronunciation, uneven breath, body tension), which present a body at the point of failing. I would argue that Simone also captures a real voice through the piano, which she uses to communicate overwhelming, unrestrained emotion even though her classically trained playing is actually quite controlled. Furthermore, a real voice emerges through the friction between her faltering command of the language and the work she put in to overcome her fear of mispronouncing words. As Jordan Stein so beautifully argues in his analysis of another of Simone's covers, "Stars," "the details of a life do not have to be literal to be real, and what Simone expresses here so powerfully is a truth that's more emotional than in any other way actual. She voices that emotional truth, she commands it and submits to it. In doing so, Simone gets to be herself, even if the song's protagonist isn't, or isn't merely."[53]

However, as Müller demonstrates, a listener's emotional state and positionality influence how they identify with the singer.[54] On the one hand, listeners may empathize with Simone's emotions because they see in her their own experiences with sadness, loss, and despair. Many Black listeners living in anti-Black spaces can particularly relate to this. Dionne Brand attributes Black music's power to how it "leaves you open, and up in the air and that this is the space that some of us need, an opening to another life tangled up in this one but opening."[55] Simone was particularly adept at and focused on drawing listeners into their emotions, as Bettina Judd shows in her analysis of Simone's 1968 tribute to the recently assassinated Martin Luther King Jr. Simone warned the audience, "You better stop and think and feel again."[56] On the other hand, listeners may derive hidden pleasure from appropriating the pain of another without actually having to live that pain, much like how white audiences often consume Black pain.[57] A documented history of white pleasure gleaned from performances of Black pain asks us to reflect on the racial implications in how various listeners identify with the realness of Simone's voice.[58]

Regardless of audience reception, Simone's own words allude to how she achieved realness and authenticity through "Ne me quitte pas." In her interview with Ardisson, Simone recounts a face-to-face experience with Brel: "I saw Jacques Brel one time in the elevator in Geneva, Switzerland, and he said, 'I'm happy that you are singing my song.'"[59] Simone displays pride in knowing that she did Brel's song justice in his eyes. This recognition offers her a sense of belonging, acknowledging shared ownership of the song and her ability to infuse it with her own authentic autobiographical perspective.

A Journey through Song

"Ne me quitte pas" would have a huge impact on Simone's journey. As she wrote in her autobiography, "I'd started to learn French when I was in Switzerland and had been performing in French for many years—the day I discovered the songs of Jacques Brel was one of the most exciting in my whole life—so Paris seemed to make sense. . . . Paris also has a wonderful African community, containing people from every country on the continent, so I would be able to create my own Africa in the heart of Europe,

Africa in my mind."[60] Just as hearing Simone's music had a life-altering effect on me, hearing Brel for the first time had a lasting effect on hers. This short passage shows how "Ne me quitte pas" was instrumental in her learning French, her moving to France, and surprisingly, her connection to Africa.

In her interview with Ardisson, Simone remarks how "this song is loved in Morocco, Senegal, and all the French-speaking countries."[61] By pinpointing francophone African countries, she speaks to the song's global appeal, which crosses geographic and racial boundaries. These crossings also indicate how artists and performers summon collectivity, or what José Esteban Muñoz calls a "brown commons," in which racially minoritized people exude a type of affect that "address[es] a sense of being-in-common as it is transmitted, across people, place, and spaces."[62] Given her protest music and her focus on Africa, Simone has participated in a sort of transatlantic Black or African commons throughout most of her career. However, because of France's colonial past, "Ne me quitte pas" allows her to reach a diverse francophone African audience bound by language and history.

Having lived in Switzerland, France, Liberia, Barbados, and the United States, Simone was no stranger to crossing borders. While each of these locations presented their own challenges, they also offered benefits she wanted. Paris, for a while, seemed particularly suited to addressing her needs. Her reflection shows an affinity for France partially spurred by the racialized contexts in both France, where she not only saw Paris as her "own Africa in the heart of Europe"[63] but could speak openly about American racism, and the United States, where her fight for racial justice had taken its toll. European fans "raved about her unique ability to evoke 'the shame' of American racial violence with her 'burning political discourse.'"[64] Just like the American-born French dancer, singer, and actress Josephine Baker before her, Simone was drawn to what France seemed to offer: respite from racial violence. I would add, though, that Europeans take advantage of the vitriolic US racial situation to downplay Europe's own long and enduring history of racial violence. In the end, Simone would have an extremely complicated relationship with Paris and would later refer to the city as her "fall from grace, a sort of punishment."[65]

Regardless, the francophone world, and especially France, remains an important piece of Simone's story. She expresses surprise when remarking, "I started to study the song to make it a hit in America. I had no idea that the French would like me for it.... The French loved me for singing that song."[66] In other words, a song she wanted to share with an American audience resonates with her fans abroad, who, for the most part, appreciate her decision to sing it in their native language, even if she couldn't pronounce the words perfectly. She succeeds because she convincingly channels the anguish and desperation of Brel's songwriting through her own lived experiences.

Although she only met him in passing, Brel's music brought so much value to Simone's life that his death devastated her. She poignantly shares with Ardisson her reaction to the news: "If Jacques Brel is gone then I don't want to stay around much longer with the world the way it is.... And I think of it too much. I did not know you were going to bring up this question.... He had an extraordinary talent. He was a great man. And I wish I could've known him personally. That's all I'm going to say about that." Ten years have passed between Brel's death and the interview, yet her retelling shows its lasting impact. She seemingly chides Ardisson for surprising her with the question "Can you explain to us why you chose this song?" What might seem like a benign inquiry forces Simone to confront emotions that remain raw even with the passage of time. But even though speaking about Brel for too long is difficult for her, she pays her respects in other ways: "When her friend Jacques Brel died, [Simone] sang his 'Ne me quitte pas,' crossing the stage at Avery Fisher [Hall] holding one note. The 14-foot train of her white gown seemed dull by comparison, but was an integral part of the act, of the homage."[67] In singing Brel's words back to him, she implores him to leave neither her nor the world—an impossible ask that lives up to the impossibilities enunciated in the lyrics.

Concluding Thoughts

While Brel enjoyed international acclaim that saw his music travel to anglophone spaces such as the United States, it took a Black American woman's cover to break through where he couldn't reach. Her audiences, especially in the sixties at the height of her Black protest music period, were undoubtedly distinctive from those listeners most attracted to chanson music. Simone's cover also facilitates linguistic travel by bringing the French language to English speakers, thus demonstrating how the act of comprehending words is only one facet of understanding a song. At the same time, francophone audiences relate differently to her performance than to Brel's because of how they may read her Blackness, her Americanness, her womanness, and her linguistic abilities. Preserving the original lyrics permits a transcendence of gender expectations. Using nonstandard pronunciation and the occasional English word demonstrates how a francophone European form of cultural production becomes recontextualized in a global market.

Furthermore, singing a song of pain and despair while Black compels listeners to consider to what extent Simone performs a real voice in a song written from the perspective of a white francophone man. On the one hand, surface-level issues like her pronunciation or her Blackness might impede her ability to capture the song's supposed real voice. On the other hand, Simone does more than simply sing the lyrics; she also claims ownership and realness through embodied emotions, evident by "Ne me quitte pas" becoming one of her iconic standards. Brel conveys the struggle enshrined in the lyrics through profuse sweating, intense facial expressions, rich vocal timbre, and a possible autobiographic connection. While there is some overlap in how

Simone demonstrates struggle, most notably through her vocal timbre, she distinguishes herself from Brel, particularly in the 1971 live performance: in how her piano playing chafes against the constraining accompaniment; in the self-consciousness of her French and the labor expended to improve it; in her strategic use of English; and in her attempts to exist as a socially conscious, classically trained Black pianist in an industry and world that didn't know what to make of her. Simone uses all the aspects of her existence—her lived experiences and embodied emotions—to guide the listener on a journey that travels on the waves of affect.

Because Simone's performance works on so many levels, anyone listening can feel a sense of belonging and imagine themselves as the intended audience. Moreover, embodying this song allows Simone to reach and embrace the francophone world. Furthermore, Simone achieves *trans + latio* through how her version—most likely the 1965 single—becomes the genesis of other covers, such as Lauryn Hill's, which was recorded for the album *Nina Revisited . . . A Tribute to Nina Simone* and performed at Simone's 2018 Rock and Roll Hall of Fame induction ceremony.[68] In this homage that enshrines Simone in the rock and roll pantheon, Brel's single is no longer the source text. Through Hill, Simone carries this song across to the next generation.

▶ **03** "We'll Sail on the Sun"

Rod McKuen and Shirley Bassey Translate Hope in a Song about Despair

IN A CLIP FROM THE last installment of the BBC4's six-episode *Shirley Bassey Show* in 1976, Rod McKuen introduces Bassey, who takes the stage in a long black dress adorned with a single silver broach.[1] As she sings the first line of "If You Go Away," a live studio audience cheers with recognition.[2] A hush then falls over the crowd, seemingly entranced by Bassey's powerful performance. When she bows her head after the final note, the raucous applause is deafening.

I encountered this song years after I became enamored with Jacques Brel's and Nina Simone's versions of "Ne me quitte pas." While I understood the crowd's enthusiasm for Bassey's riveting performance, my knowledge of the original and Simone's cover tempered my response. Critics have generally disapproved of English translations of Brel's oeuvre, "highlight[ing] rather disparagingly the difficulty of translating lyrics faithfully, and of reproducing Brel's own powerful stage performances and vocal delivery."[3] While there are probably few anglophone singers who are more impressive performers than Dame Bassey, the English lyrics arguably lack the gravitas of the original French, making it difficult for anyone familiar with the two versions to hold the songs in the same regard.

Regardless, there is much interest in Brel and this song in the anglophone world. Of the "big three" chanson artists, Brel is the most internationally recognized, not only because he occasionally performed abroad but also because of how his work circulated: "His songs, translated into English, were those that travelled best.[4] According to *Chorus* magazine, Brel even received a 'Special Citation of Achievement' to reward the fact that the American adaptation of his song *Ne me quitte pas* (*If you go away* in English) was broadcast over a million times in the United States."[5] From Frank Sinatra to Cyndi Lauper, Neil Diamond, and Barbra Streisand, it seems that every established English-singing performer wants their chance to convey the devastating story Brel created. It has also been performed in nearly thirty languages, including Dutch, German, Hebrew, Italian, Japanese, Russian, and Spanish.[6] The song's popularity highlights the importance of translation in transnational cultural production, demonstrating that even seemingly inadequate translations can have a profound effect on the new audiences they reach.

Translation and Music

Translation is the process of taking a text from a source language and creating a new, similar text in a target language. This new text is not an exact replica of the original meaning and feel, especially when translating literary or artistic texts: "Translating rewrites a source text in terms that are intelligible and interesting to receptors, situating it in different patterns of language use, in different literary traditions, in different cultural values, in different social institutions, and often in a different historical moment."[7] If "If You Go Away" is indeed the product of transforming "Ne me quitte pas" from a song that captures the "nightmare of relinquishing one's last shred of self-respect" into "a song which most [Anglophones] know as a sweet love song," it's because English-speaking audiences resonate with this transformed message.[8] In many ways, "If You Go Away" is a transcreation, a term that highlights the need to "capture the cultural meanings and emotional nuances that resist direct translation, enabling them to be recognized in a new context."[9] Transcreation centers the creative aspects of the translation process and emphasizes the concept of making something new.

Much of translation theory has focused on what gets lost in translation because, as critiques of song translations demonstrate, listeners who understand the lyrics of both versions notice meaningful changes.[10] But audiences unfamiliar with "Ne me quitte pas" have no knowledge of the meanings and emotions of the French version. Nothing is lost. They experience the affective qualities of this new version and engage with it on its own terms. Translations, like covers, are destined for different audiences, which provide a song the opportunity for tremendous gain, such as increased geographic reach. Lawrence Venuti remarks, "In the case of foreign texts that have achieved mass circulation, a translation becomes the site of unexpected groupings, fostering communities of readers who would otherwise be separated by cultural differences and social divisions yet are now joined by a common fascination."[11] In other words, translations break down borders and allow texts to travel between people of various, often disparate, communities, forging a new translinguistic community through a common bond with the text. Someone in France could be humming the same tune as someone in America without having heard the same song.

Susan Bassnett takes this travel metaphor even further by comparing translation to human movement: "Today the movement of peoples around the globe can be seen to mirror the very process of translation itself, for translation is not just the transfer of texts from one language into another, it is now rightly seen as a process of negotiation between texts and between cultures, a process during which all kinds of transactions take place mediated by the figure of the translator."[12] Referring to the translator as a liberator "who frees the text from the fixed signs of its original shape," Bassnett flags the translator's agency and power in transcending geographic, cultural, and generational barriers to give a text new life and opportunities: "The translation effectively becomes the after-life of a text, a new 'original' in another language. This positive view of translation serves to reinforce the importance of translating as an act both of inter-cultural and inter-temporal communication."[13] As such, translations do not just travel geographically outward through space but generationally through time. Importantly, fandom of songs in foreign languages drives the need for translations, and today's technologies make it easy for anyone to offer them.[14] The popularity of songs, their accessibility, and the ease with which they travel make them ripe for *trans + latio*, for being carried across space and time.

While translators wield power, they also bear responsibility and must contend with a myriad of issues. Song translations cause practical difficulties because translators not only have to convey meaning but also deal with such structural constraints as rhythm and rhyme. All speech has rhythm to it, but its importance is heightened in music. Since lyrics are inextricably linked to melodic rhythm, singable translations must adhere to the rhythm of the original or risk losing their recognizability as an afterlife of that text. For many, rhythm is the top requisite in creating good song translations.[15] Preserving rhyme (if the source material rhymes) is somewhat important, but conveying a similar feel to the rhyming in the original can be more effective than replicating the exact rhyme scheme.[16] Preserving meaning is also a consideration but not necessarily the primarily goal.[17]

Translators engage in a balancing act in what has been described as "a pentathlete trying to optimize his score over five dissimilar 'events': namely Singability, Sense, Naturalness, Rhythm and Rhyme."[18] This dissimilarity makes translation of music so difficult because each facet requires a different skill set, and adherence to one criterion may impede the ability to succeed at another. Whereas translation scholars such as Venuti argue for a strategy of foreignization where preserving meaning often comes at the expense of target-language expectations, translators of song may prefer the strategy of domestication, which can result in drastic deviations from the source text, particularly regarding meaning.[19] The wide range of considerations a song translator must weigh puts in perspective negative critiques of "If You Go Away" that focus specifically on the sense of the lyrics and its uneasy relationship to the music's emotional color. While translation theory tends to focus on literary texts and the slippage between source text and target culture, analyzing songs and their translations offers a way to place the focus on mobility and the far-reaching afterlives of texts.

A Translation Tradition

The translation of "Ne me quitte pas" doesn't happen in a vacuum but belongs to a legacy of texts moving across languages and geographies. Several well-known English songs were originally French, unbeknownst to anglophone audiences. Frank Sinatra's rendition of "My Way" wouldn't exist without Claude François's "Comme d'habitude" (As usual). The same goes for Bobby Darin's "Beyond the Sea" (from Charles Trenet's "La mer" [The sea]) and Louis Armstrong's English version of Édith Piaf's "La vie en rose" (Life in pink). These versions sound musically like the originals, especially with regard to melody and rhythm, but fidelity of lyrics varies considerably.

The French lyrics of "La vie en rose" by Piaf and the English translation by Mack David are probably the most similar, particularly in tone. Both recount how beautiful life is when being embraced by a lover, and the English translation even preserves the refrain in French. However, there are subtle differences in perspective. While both are written in first person, the French version describes the narrator's lover in third person (*il* [he]), while the English version uses second person (you). Also, Armstrong's English version omits the first section of the original lyrics, opting for a long instrumental instead. This instrumental section allows Armstrong to showcase his trumpet, which de-emphasizes the lyrics but heightens the music's emotional resonance.

Both "La mer" and "Beyond the Sea" speak about the sea, but they take different lyrical approaches. Trenet's "La mer" personifies the dancing sea that rocks the narrator's heart, and the lyrics evoke natural and spiritual images (e.g., rain, sky, sheep, shepherds, angels, birds). This is a love song, according to the last verse, but not one intended for a specific person. Meanwhile, Albert Lasry and Jack Lawrence's translation, "Beyond the Sea," uses similar natural imagery (e.g., birds, sands, stars, moon), but the sea is more a backdrop for the ode to the narrator's far-off lover and their future reunion. The tone is one of longing for a person instead of admiration for a place. However, the music and associated emotions give similar vibes.

When Paul Anka penned new lyrics to "My Way," he preserved structural aspects, such as rhythm, but completely rewrote the sense and sentiment. He transformed a song written in future tense, depicting the daily habits of a romantic relationship on its last legs, into an end-of-life reflection written primarily in past tense, chronicling a life without regret. However, in listening to Claude François's and Frank Sinatra's versions side by side without paying attention to the lyrics, one might never know how unalike they are.

"My Way" underwent further resignification when British bassist Sid Vicious and German singer Nina Hagen each released punk versions about a decade later. Both versions completely disregard the iconicity of the originals. In addition to conveying different lyrical emotions, the music elicits a distinctive emotional response driven by the punk genre. Furthermore, Hagen's mix of English and German adds another layer of linguistic border-crossing. These examples provide insight into how translators and performers interpret lyrics and how they move a song from one linguistic and cultural environment to another. They also highlight the expectations listeners may or may not have regarding the translation of emotion and meaning from French-language source material.

In all three of the above examples, as well as in Brel's "Ne me quitte pas," the lyricist is the one who makes the French versions popular. The French term *auteur-compositeur-interprète*, which is central to chanson and other forms of French popular music, differs from the English translation singer-songwriter, which elides the importance of performance. *Interprète* can be translated as "musician" or "performer" when speaking about music but as "interpreter" when talking about oral translation. Indeed, there is a certain interpretation of meaning and emotion that happens when lifting the words from the page. As an *interprète*, the owner of the words is in a unique position to transmit the vision they had when writing the song. In thinking about how adept Brel was at bringing his own lyrics alive, I cannot help but wonder what it was like for him to translate the significance of his own texts during his performances and how this process differed from McKuen linguistically translating lyrics for Bassey to perform.

McKuen and Bassey:
Interpreters Extraordinaires

McKuen, an American poet and singer-songwriter, met Brel in Paris during the 1960s. McKuen translated several of Brel's works, including major hits "Seasons in the Sun" ("Le moribund") and "If You Go Away," which allowed Brel's music to readily travel to anglophone spaces. However, McKuen's translation and writing abilities are often disparaged. As an obituary of McKuen notes, "A 1967 *Time* magazine article characterized his poetry as nothing but 'sweet love, lonely rooms, silent rain, quiet snow, and lost cats.' A *Newsweek* critic called him the 'king of kitsch.'"[20] Nevertheless, McKuen was prolific and successful, writing more than fifteen hundred songs and selling more than one hundred million musical recordings.[21] Some of the biggest names in the business—Johnny Cash, Barbra Streisand, Frank Sinatra, and of course Shirley Bassey—sang his songs.

While many view McKuen's translations of Brel's work as disappointing imitations, some scholars and journalists offer a more favorable analysis. Chris Tinker notes that both "Seasons in the Sun" and "If You Go Away" "highlight some of the specificities of the French chanson form: the foregrounding of lyrics; the honesty and intensity of emotion; and a readiness to tackle death more explicitly and extensively than in Anglophone popular music."[22] Matt Schudel describes McKuen as Brel's close friend and "an English-language version of the French chansonnier, a combination of songwriter, singer and bard."[23] This depiction suggests that McKuen convincingly embodied the French notion of *auteur-compositeur-interprète* and went beyond the confines of the anglophone notion of singer-songwriter.

McKuen's own reflections on his artistic relationship with Brel provide insight into how he positioned himself in the world of chanson and in Brel's sphere: "As friends and as musical collaborators we had traveled, toured, and written—together and apart—the events of our lives as if they were songs, and I guess they were. When news of Jacques' death came, I stayed locked in my bedroom and drank for a week. That kind of self-pity was something he wouldn't have approved of, but all I could do was replay our songs (our children) and ruminate over our unfinished life together."[24] These emotions echo Simone's encounter with the news of Brel's passing. It appears McKuen found that the best way to honor his friend and respect Brel's craft was by writing deeply affective and moving translations of his work that were authentic to McKuen's own sensibilities. In other words, while many critics see unsatisfactory translations, his fans highly regard these texts for their merit as poetic, emotionally charged works of art.[25] In the "carried across" sense of translation, McKuen's work was an overwhelming success because he brought audiences the essence of Brel while also transforming Brel's oeuvre into something that stands on its own. McKuen's domesticating strategy for translating songs is part of what allows them to travel so well.[26]

One of the reasons McKuen's translations succeed is because of artists like Shirley Bassey, who bring his words alive through a variety of performance elements. In many ways, Bassey is a perfect fit for McKuen's vision of "If You Go Away" because she pairs the dramatic, sappy lyrics with equally melodramatic facial and bodily expressions. A critique of Bassey from 1959 marvels, "She not only has vocal appeal but tremendous artistry. Every flick of the wrist, each flutter of the eyelashes and every pout, adds to the selling of her songs."[27] McKuen would agree. When he introduces Bassey on her variety show, McKuen describes this song as "a favorite song of mine, because I wrote it, and because nobody sings it like you do."[28] He is even more effusive in a letter to her in 1967 soon after receiving the test pressing of her album *And We Were Lovers*. Expressing his gratitude, he writes, "I am unwinding and next to me is that probing, prying voice of yours—now warm, now cold as an iceberg, coaxing out my song and a brilliant program of other tunes. Thank you for singing 'If You Go Away.' Thank you for doing something different with it."[29] It's possible that McKuen had Bassey in mind when translating "Ne me quitte pas," and it's obvious he believed that with this single she made the song her own.

Not every critique of Bassey is as effusive as McKuen's. Many focus on how her physicality seems to drown out her voice. For instance, a review of Bassey's show at the London Palladium in 1962 offers the following backhanded compliment: "She more than deserves her success, if only for the enthusiasm she injects into her act, and the pulsating, pressurised pace with which she delivers the goods. If her voice isn't as mellow toned as other singers, what she lacks in quality is more than adequately compensated for by the quantity. Her hands are beautifully expressive and her whole soul is projected into her every number."[30] According to this critic, her delivery, expression, and ability to project her whole soul makes up for subpar vocals. Meanwhile, a critic who saw her perform at the Greek Theatre in Los Angeles in 1976 states that "the Basseyistics get a little carried away."[31] In doing so, he coins an eponymous term to describe her theatrics. Performative gestures have become synonymous with her name.

However, the use of animal imagery is the most striking theme in critiques of Bassey. Sometimes it's subtle, such as when the same critic remarks, "Slithering in hot pink sequins and pearls, Bassey has her glamour role down tight.... Bassey remains a foremost chanteuse."[32] While no animal is openly mentioned, "slithering" conjures the image of a snake and evokes a biblical nod to temptation and its gendered implications. At the same time, "chanteuse" positions Bassey in the chanson genre with Simone.

Other examples are more explicit in their animal references. Several throughout the years have referred to her as a tigress, a play on her hometown of Tiger Bay in Cardiff, Wales. Similarly, a 1957 article implied animalistic movement: "Shirley Bassey—the tigress from Tiger Bay—glides on to the stage."[33] In 1963 a critic in New York remarked, "A tawny tigress . . . exciting and intense."[34]

Instead of tying the animal image to movement, this one underscores her color, most likely hinting at her biracial background as the daughter of a white English mother and Black Nigerian father. A 1970 review from Melbourne, Australia, more obviously highlighted the interplay of racial undertones and animal imagery when referring to Bassey as a "dusky thrush."[35] They went on to argue that "far too many of the ballads are rendered in the loud Bassey belting manner, so that they become monotonously repetitive, and one longs for some calmer contrast and perhaps pointed numbers. They all seem to be over-dramatized."[36]

While few of the reviews I encounter explicitly refer to Bassey's race, the chromatic hints and reliance on animal imagery suggest an underlying racialized discourse that intersects with gender considerations. In discussing "fetishized and animalized sexual imagery," Joy James notes how "racial and sexual caricatures corseting the female black body have a strong historical legacy."[37] Both the critiques of Bassey's supposed animallike qualities and the attention placed on her appearance serve to strip the singer of her humanity. The former suggests she's unrefined, while the latter questions her ability to feel and convey emotions.[38] These perceptions can influence the extent to which an audience reads realness in a voice and how successfully a song's interpreter can bring out the essence of a text. As the following pages show, Bassey's embodiment of the song through her performance aligns with McKuen's text to create a moving rendition, even though its emotional resonance differs from Brel's and Simone's versions.

Experiencing the Text

The Lyrics

> *We'll sail (on) the sun*
> *We'll ride on the rain*
> *We'll talk to the trees*
> *And worship the wind*

Comparing "If You Go Away" with the original sheds light on the nature of musical translation from how translators and performers capture the spirit of the original to how translation allows a song to travel. McKuen's lyrics convey a very different sentiment from Brel's.[39] The most immediately noticeable change is to the title and refrain—the desperate imperative of "Ne me quitte pas" (Don't leave me) becomes a conditional phrase suggesting hope in "If You Go Away." The beginning of the song also establishes a more positive tone through images of the sun, birds, new love, and high hearts, a marked contrast with the depiction of forgetfulness, lost time, and misunderstandings in the first verse of the original. While this positive imagery doesn't fully negate the song's displays of sadness and loss—for instance, the third verse describes a world standing still and a narrator dying slowly, and the fifth depicts overwhelming emptiness—its proliferation in McKuen's version tempers the hints of devastation. The choice of perspective makes the tone further diverge from the original, as seen in the second verse when the narrator uses a series of *we* phrases to paint a shared future instead of the *je* (I) Brel uses to lay out all the impossible feats the narrator promises to do for their lover. The projection of *we* suggests the ability to imagine a successful relationship, while the lack of *nous* (we) in all of "Ne me quitte pas" conveys a sense of antagonism instead of camaraderie, obsession instead of love.

In addition to a brighter tone, McKuen's translation effaces some of the intricacies of Brel's rhetorical devices. "If You Go Away" lacks the obvious references to high culture so evident in "Ne me quitte pas" (e.g., Stendhal, Dostoevsky). Chanson distinguishes itself from other genres through its ability to blur distinctions between high culture and popular culture.[40] In creating a pop standard in the Anglo-American tradition, McKuen was less motivated to capture these literary flourishes.[41] He makes overtures to the original imagery but in a more static way. The descriptions of taking the sun away or birds flying in the summer sky come across as flat when compared to Brel's action-packed "ciel flamboie," "terres brulées," "rejaillir le feu de l'ancien volcan," "leurs coeurs s'embraser" (blazing sky, scorched earth, old spurting volcano, their hearts ablaze). Similarly, the notion of oblivion in an "empty room" and "empty space" pales in comparison to "oublier ces heures qui tuaient parfois" (forget the hours that would sometimes kill).

For his part, McKuen employs other types of rhetorical devices that imbue the song with a poetic element. The most salient is his reliance on alliteration in the lines "We'll sail (on) the sun, we'll ride on the rain, we'll talk to the trees, and worship the wind."[42] The pleasing sound of these repetitive consonants resonates in a way that elicits an emotional response from the listener. It also appears to speed up time as the words roll off the tongue, alluding to quickening breaths. I would argue, however, that McKuen's more poetic contributions don't come close to the sheer beauty of Brel's imagery, such as fan favorite "des perles de pluie venues de pays où il ne pleut pas" (pearls of rain coming from countries where it doesn't rain), which is not only highly alliterative but descriptively complex as well. Simply put, McKuen's lyrics lack the intensity and artistry of Brel's.

The same critique can be made of the lyrics' structure. The rhymes are loose, relying on matching vowel sounds instead of true rhymes. The lack of rigidity conveys less intensity. The more subdued emotional charge is particularly apparent in the last verse. While the line "shadow of your shadow" is arguably the only literal translation in the whole song (i.e., "l'ombre de ton ombre") and therefore stands out, McKuen stops short of fully engaging with Brel's overwhelming image of desperation by not translating "l'ombre de ton chien" (the shadow of your dog). Instead, he goes directly into the line "if I had thought it might have kept me by your side." McKuen's decision fits the overall tone of his song but diverges from the original intent of Brel's, reminding us that translation isn't about faithfully re-creating the original but creating a new text that brings the audience on a different journey.

The Music

While McKuen's drastic changes to the lyrics' sentiment results in what I consider a more lackluster version, the subtle changes made to the music are more effective in conveying emotional intensity. He mostly keeps the same melody but with a few important changes. The line jumps an octave at "when the day was young" and remains an octave higher throughout the refrain until "or will be again." Perhaps McKuen imagined a female singer—nothing in his lyrics specifies gender, unlike in the original—and modified the music to showcase a higher vocal range. The move to a higher octave infuses energy into the music and builds intensity. This jump also corresponds with the word "high" in the first verse, demonstrating how the music reflects the sentiment of the lyrics.

McKuen also slightly modifies the melody's rhythm. While for most of the song he stays faithful to the four eighth note / one quarter note rhythm Brel employs, in the second and fourth verses McKuen liberally inserts syncopated triplets starting in the line "I'll make you a day" and "I'll make you a night," respectively. He then returns to the original duple rhythm for a couple of measures until the aforementioned lines "We'll sail the sun, we'll ride on the rain, we'll talk to the trees, and worship the wind" in the second verse and "I'll sail on your smile, I'll ride on your touch, I'll talk to your eyes, that I love so much" in the fourth. After a few more measures of the original rhythm, McKuen ends these verses with one more triplet. This syncopation not only breaks up the rhythmic monotony but emphasizes the litany of offerings the narrator bestows on their lover. The syncopation infuses the melody with a type of movement that works in tandem with the lyrics' imagery (e.g., motion verbs in "sail [on] the sun," "ride on the rain," "sail on your smile," "ride on your touch"). The flow of the syncopation also enhances the rhythm of the alliteration. The rhythmic complexity arguably mimics a fluttering heart or a shivering exhalation.

Furthermore, McKuen takes liberties with the song's harmony. The lyrics offer hope instead of despair, and the harmony uses major chords to crystalize this hope. For instance, in the lines "All the birds that flew . . . the night was long," McKuen composes the same melodic notes as in the original but cocoons them in major chords, which conveys a brighter, more positive tone than Brel's corresponding minor chords. McKuen then builds tension in the first appearance of the refrain by using complex chords (e.g., sixth chords, seventh chords, and slash chords) instead of triads, which highlights the ambiguous emotions inherent in the meaning of "if you go away." Because of the conditional "if," we don't know what the lover will decide, leaving the door open for a possible rekindling of love.

The Performance

The lyrics and music of "If You Go Away" lack the emotional despair of the original, but Shirley Bassey's incredible vocal ability and stage presence make her performance on the *Shirley Bassey Show* as memorable as Brel's and Simone's "Ne me quitte pas." She is an expert at facial expressions and mannerisms, just like Brel, and her approach to this song gestures to him. But in many ways her performance and goals are distinctive.

She begins with her eyes closed and slowly raises her head before opening them at the end of the first line. She then alternates between opened and closed eyes. When her eyes are open, she moves her eyeballs from side to side in a somewhat disarming way. She also sways her head back and forth, and even when she's not singing she moves her lips at the end of lines in a pantomimed expression. As with Brel, these exaggerated movements draw the audience in, allowing them to deeply experience the moment. However, they don't have the same emotional resonance as those of Brel, who seems intent on convincing you he is the narrator. Bassey comes across as more interested in putting on a good show than in making you believe her.

In addition to the mannerisms, Bassey also plays with volume, tempo, and vocal quality in ways similar to Brel, though not as drastically. Like Brel, she launches into the second verse at a higher volume than the first, which reinforces the positivity of that verse's lyrics. She also draws out notes, although at different moments than Brel. For instance, she builds up the tension when she lengthens *go* in "but if you go" and then hangs even longer on the syllable *un* in "understand." The sheer acoustic power, the quality of her vibrato, and the impressive control of her voice leave the listener speechless. This contrast to the breathy whisper of *love* and *hand* in the following lines mimics the emotional ebb and flow of the lyrics with its opposing *if/but* structure. Bassey then sings two lines of the refrain without blinking, enhancing the slowing of time achieved by the lengthening of notes at the end of the second verse. Throughout the song she also intersperses audible breaths, and she draws attention to certain words by accentuating consonants (e.g., the *l* at the end of *well*). Bassey defies critics who complain about her lack of mellow tone and vocal contrast.

While these musical decisions enhance the dramatic effect, Bassey also makes some subtle changes to the written lyrics, slightly modifying the meaning of the translation, the relationship to Brel's original, and the listeners' response to the performance. In McKuen's lyrics *I* statements dominate the fourth verse, unlike the second verse, which is replete with *we* statements. In Bassey's 1976 live performance, she uses *we* statements in both the second and fourth verses (e.g., "we'll sail on your smile," "we'll ride on your touch"), which intensifies the bond between the narrator and their lover, and between the singer and her audience. However, the most striking modification Bassey makes is at the very end, when instead of singing "the shadow of your shadow," she reinserts Brel's dog figure with "the shadow of your dog."[43] This decision thus reintroduces the gravitas and debasement of Brel's original and offers a counterexample to performers such as Barbara. Perhaps Bassey chooses to include it as a sly reference to the animalizing perspectives on her performances, or as an homage to Brel's original, or maybe to stay true to what I see as her primary concern: performing drama convincingly. Regardless of the reasons for her lyrical changes and performance decisions, Bassey demonstrates her role as an *interprète*—a translator of sorts.

Dramatizing Realness

In our class discussion and reflection papers comparing "Ne me quitte pas" and "If You Go Away," my students tapped into the emotional impact of the songs, noted the stylistic changes, and ruminated on technical aspects of translation in thoughtful ways. As French majors in an American-based classroom, most gravitated toward either Brel's or Simone's because of how it connected with their career aspirations. One student even flat-out disliked Bassey's version for what she described as a bad translation. Regardless, most enjoyed what Bassey accomplished through her artistry and through McKuen's storytelling. One student appreciated "If You Go Away" because it was romantic and poetic, a true love song. Another preferred the English version because it was easier to connect with the meaning. For her, music had more depth when you understood the nuances and emotions tied to the word as opposed to just the literal translation. Since she could only scratch the surface with the original French, she felt she was missing its full power. Still another student was drawn to Bassey's version because of nostalgia. It reminded her of her grandmother, who used to listen to Bassey on repeat. They all connected to the song differently depending on their expectations and lived experiences. Their responses provide insight into the various ways consumers of music engage with songs.

There is no doubt that Bassey is the consummate performer, evidenced by how she stages her emotions, exudes self-awareness, and pays close attention to her voice. Her approach is similar to Müller's reading of British singer-songwriter Kate Bush's "Feel It," in which they contend that listeners "encounter the vocal sound as an aesthetic object clearly separable from the vocalic body."[44] Arguing that Bush employs nothing close to a "real" voice, Müller likens it to a mask, in which "the artificiality of a mask is beyond doubt, and it would never be mistaken for something real. . . . In contrast to the 'real' voice, the subject does not show its emotionality in its voice, but 'hides' behind obviously false and artificial vocal clichés."[45] Similarly, Bassey seems to rely on overemphasis, which coaxes the listener to fixate on the surface level of the singing style and the sound instead of identifying with how the singer feels. She pairs this aural exaggeration with mannerisms. As a caption to a 1963 photo of Bassey describes, "Mocking innocence, Shirley displays inexhaustible stock of facial expressions."[46] Brel is known for dramatic overemphasis as well but in a way that leaves the listener thinking they've been handed a piece of his soul. Bassey also bares her soul but does so to leave the listener with a carefully crafted depiction of an emotion instead of the emotion itself. Both experiences touch the listener deeply while showing the range of goals performers strive to achieve.

However, when I compare "If You Go Away" with "Ne me quitte pas," I'm most cognizant of myself as a Black woman watching two iconic Black women who experience race and gender differently. According to biographical accounts, Bassey avoided the racialized violence so prevalent in Simone's life. Bassey has indicated she was oblivious to racism as a mixed-race child in 1940s Britain.[47] Free from the toll of constant discrimination, Bassey could imagine capaciously what she wanted from her life. She became enamored with the idea of stardom when her sister took her to a Billy Eckstine concert, where she witnessed the mesmerizing effects the jazz singer had over the crowd. By the 1960s, Bassey had become the glamorous voice of the James Bond franchise, with "Goldfinger" in 1965 and "Diamonds Are Forever" in 1971. During the same time, Simone was singing protest music under the United States' repressive Jim Crow laws.

Known for her high slits, plunging necklines, furs, and jewelry, Bassey cultivated an image akin to a carefree Bond girl as Simone got blacklisted for speaking truth to power. Bassey seemed unencumbered by social conceptualizations of Blackness. However, just because Bassey took a color-blind approach doesn't mean her Blackness didn't inform her career and life paths. As Andy Medhurst argues, "The indignities of making her West End debut in a British revue called *Hot from Harlem* or of having a first hit record with the colonial kitsch of 'Banana Boat Song' (all this in the era of the Notting Hill riots) are memories that surely fuel the conviction with which she sings of transcending adversity."[48] And as evidenced by coded language in reviews of her work, others noticed her Blackness. Furthermore, even though Bassey has spent a lifetime cultivating a diva persona, she doesn't fit neatly into what many imagine as feminine: "She's tough as old boots, her success driven by a strength and single-mindedness that sits uneasily with social expectations of the feminine. Asked in the BBC film why her romantic relationships with men tended to founder, she said, wistfully but without a trace of regret, that she 'was not fragile enough.'"[49] Bassey's presentation of race and gender defies expectations.

In many ways, this approach to race and gender is reflected in her role as a performer. The masking of her real voice, as Müller would describe it, allows Bassey to control what others see of her and feel from her music. Signaling her "highly attuned grasp of camp," Medhurst contends that "nobody parodies her excessive theatricality better than herself."[50] This ability for subversion is a reason Bassey has had such a huge following in queer spaces, especially in drag performance (something I explore in detail in chapter 4).

Concluding Thoughts

Comparing the McKuen/Bassey pairing with the Brel and Simone versions demonstrates the different ways a song allows listeners to travel to and within an affective space. While McKuen wrote a memorable song, for many people the lyrics fail to capture Brel's heartrending sentiment. However, the chasm between the connotations of "don't leave me" and "if you go away" calls into question whether the English version is a translation or if it is better described as a derivation, a transcreation, or an adaptation. It's evident McKuen used translation to bring the audience on a different emotional journey than Brel did. Even though English is my first language, my own emotional response to the English version will never rise to the level of what I feel when listening to the French versions. I would posit that for most English-French bilinguals, the emotional resonance of the French version greatly eclipses that of the English version, indicating the vulnerability of translations. At the same time, as this chapter and the next show, Bassey's version has had a profound and transformative effect on generations of listeners. I'm still blown away every time I hear it. I just don't expect my heart to break a little more each time like I do with "Ne me quitte pas." But would my reaction be different if I had heard this version before Simone's and Brel's?

When I first listened to "If You Go Away," I felt that Bassey's impressive performativity and vocal acuity weren't enough to overcome the emotional flatness of the lyrics. But when I reflect on the song as a work of transcreation, I realize she is in lock-step with the impact of McKuen's lyrics, which convey a Holly-woodized and therefore artificial version of lost love. As such, her performative gestures and vocal clichés allude to a mask instead of genuine emotion. In a way, both McKuen and Bassey are working within the established conventions of anglophone pop songs of this era. Bassey is also doing her own translation work. As one critic notes, "Bassey sings at the top of her passions. She translates her emotions with vocal power."[51] She therefore takes McKuen's lyrics and, through the manipulation of her voice and bodily expressions, conjures emotions her listeners can latch onto. She also uses her incredible skill to counteract any objectifying perceptions that could render her less than human. McKuen's letter to Bassey conveys the transcendent power of her single, but I find that her flamboyant live performances of "If You Go Away" are where the English translation truly shines. While translation theory usually doesn't account for performance, Bassey carries across McKuen's vision to the audience through her theatricality. Furthermore, the next chapter will show how her performance creates numerous afterlives. In sum, Bassey is the ultimate *interprète*.

Regardless of the affective limitations and distortions of the English version, the mere act of translation permits this franco-phone cultural juggernaut to enter anglophone spaces broadly. Simone's version, as a French-language song performed by a Black American woman, offers one version of a geographic and social leap. Bassey's version, an English-language song by a Black British woman, provides similar movement but also opens the possibility for anglophone audiences to travel linguistically. The way they engage with race and gender differ, but both show how people other than the original performer can claim ownership, authenticity, and emotional truthfulness. In the span of ten years, we see how a single song travels in numerous directions, multiplies, and reinvents itself. Each version profoundly affects listeners on its own terms.

▶ 04 From "Ne me quitte pas" to "If You Go Away"

Adapting Iconic Songs to Film and Stage

BREL ORDERS A BEER and watches a man sing his composition "Amsterdam" to a bawdy, dancing crowd. Near the song's end, the camera lingers on Brel as he sits alone at a table. Then we see an image of rough ocean waves followed by an extreme close-up of Brel's eyes. As the camera pans out to show Brel from the waist up, he sings "Ne me quitte pas" with a cigarette between his fingers. No one else is in this scene, a major contrast from the dancing patrons pressed against one another during the previous song. The camera then tightens again to an extreme close-up that frames only Brel's eyes.

In 1975 French-Canadian filmmaker Denis Héroux and American film producer Ely Landau brought Jacques Brel's music to the big screen through American Film Theatre (AFT). Their film was an adaptation of Eric Blau and Mort Shuman's off-Broadway musical revue *Jacques Brel Is Alive and Well and Living in Paris*, a stage adaptation of Brel's oeuvre that debuted in 1968 in New York's Greenwich Village. The original revue showcased twenty-six of Brel's songs translated into English and sung by Elly Stone, Shuman, Shawn Elliott, and Alice Whitfield.

Blau reflects on what can be gained through adaptation and translation when done well: "[Brel's] generosity, in a professional sense, is unusual. Mort and I had finished the translation of 'My Death.' It was a close transfer from the French to the English. But we thought that the music missed something. Mort, knowing Brel far better than I, said, 'I'll change the tune. He won't mind.' So Mort did and sent a tape to Jacques. Jacques' answer came: 'You've improved it. It's better than mine.'"[1] Brel's response suggests an understanding of the importance of recontextualization and how a text must transform to better reflect a new context influenced by language, culture, and audience.

While the off-Broadway show was a success, the film version flopped, partially because it wasn't in tune with audience expectations. Over two seasons AFT produced fourteen films, experimenting with how plays are adapted to film: "The directive was to take a great stage play, *not change a word*, and in most cases, use the actual play script as the screenplay. The next step was to hire an accomplished film director to interpret the text for the film medium *but stay faithful to the play*."[2] Héroux, an avant-garde filmmaker, positioned Brel as a cultured intellectual who could best be appreciated by an intellectual audience: "As Landau's wife and collaborator Edie comments . . . the AFT series was intended to appeal not to 'the lowest common denominator of audience intelligence,' but to a 'limited but important segment of the movie-going audience who had abandoned going to the movies,' who wished for an alternative to 'big action, youth-oriented' films, and who preferred 'something that a thinking person would enjoy so that they felt enriched.'"[3] The few people who appreciate this adaptation tend to identify as sophisticated, North American, and Francophile—a stark contrast to the mass appeal of Brel's music in France and to Rod McKuen's translations for the anglophone world.[4]

The harsh reviews from the time capture the many failures in the adaptation process. Likening it to "a public service for those people who somehow managed not to see the Off Broadway stage show during its nearly five-year run at the Village Gate," Vincent Canby argues that "Mr. Héroux . . . has transformed what was essentially a concert into an extravaganza of surreal images that keep messing things up. The images are vivid and disconnected to one another (good) but they inevitably wind up being visual translations of the lyrics (bad)."[5] While it comes across as somewhat classist, Canby's quip that the film brings the show to those who haven't seen the live musical speaks to the accessibility adaptation engenders. However, Héroux fell short because he was unable to convincingly adapt a stage show, which is suitable for concert-style material, to the screen, which benefits from a narrative arc. Canby is also unimpressed with what he sees as "visual translations of the lyrics," which hit the spectator over the head with literal images of the words: "All those images and the changes of scenery and costumes . . . get in the way of possible listening pleasure." Brel is renowned for his poetic lyrics and simple yet impassioned performances that captivate listeners. The film—with its disconcerting marionettes; theatrical, over-the-top acting; and gaudy decorations—buries what I find so attractive about Brel's repertoire: the raw and visceral emotion that hangs on every word and note. Adapting songs to film, much like translating songs, requires both creative risks and deep engagement with the new context without sacrificing the text's affective power.

The one triumph in the film is "Ne me quitte pas." Absent from the original stage version, this song not only appears in the film adaptation but is the only one Brel sings himself and the only one performed in the original French. Ironically, Brel's performance seems out of place in a film that uses his music as source material. This one scene makes you forget you're watching a disjointed, esoteric, clumsy adaptation of his music and transports you to what seems very much like Brel's world. "Ne me quitte pas" tethers the adaptation to the original. Héroux's choice to have Brel perform this song, and in French, reiterates how central "Ne me quitte pas" is to our understanding of the singer. In some regards, this decision suggests this song is better left unadapted. However, the rest of the chapter will show that there are many excellent adaptations of "Ne me quitte pas" whose variety demonstrates just how adeptly it crosses multiple thresholds.

Adaptation

"Ne me quitte pas" hasn't just moved from one voice to another through covering or from one language to another through translation. It has also crossed borders of media and genre to find a home in film, theatre, and various types of performance art. These border crossings require adaptation of the source text to fit in a new context through a complex process of shifting materials "to a different, multidimensional medium with different traditions, practices and conditions of production."[6] But what exactly is an adaptation, and how is it different from a cover or a translation?

Somewhat confusingly, many critics and commentators refer to "If You Go Away" as an adaptation instead of a translation. Unclear definitions contribute to the tenuous position of musical texts in translation studies: "The fuzzy boundaries between 'translation,' 'adaptation,' 'version,' 'rewriting,' etc. and the pervasiveness of covert and unacknowledged translations in music have generally limited research in this area to overt and canonized translation practices, such as those undertaken for the opera."[7] However, distinguishing between these different phenomena is not as important as analyzing these texts for insight into intercultural communication as well as social, cultural, and linguistic practices.

The field of adaptation studies dates to the mid-twentieth century, but adaptations were happening in some form long before they became the subject of scholarly inquiry. The late eighteenth-century Romantic period was when "cultural assumptions surrounding originality, adaptation, invention, derivation, art, mass culture, genre, purity, and genius emerged or shifted decisively," laying the groundwork for modern notions of textual adaptations, such as plays based on novels.[8] In cinema and media studies, film adaptation has been central from the beginning.[9] Recent work in adaptation studies has sought to decenter film adaptation and move beyond textual analysis to focus on the sociocultural contexts that produce these adaptations.[10] Timothy Corrigan notes how through a new focus on "performance studies, music, political activity, and numerous other social and cultural platforms . . . adaptation studies has emphasized the material differences and compromises that shape both the movement of texts between various media . . . and the movement of ideas, social positions, and identities between cultures, across geographical borders."[11] This scholarship offers a blueprint for how to approach the various adaptations of "Ne me quitte pas."

A film adaptation studies perspective entails the "examination of adaptations as cultural objects in their own right, distinct both from the materials they adapt and from films that do not make the adaptation of prior materials central to their signifying process."[12] However, this exploration of the new text as its own entity and an important cultural contribution doesn't mean it should be analyzed in a vacuum. Lucy Mazdon's work on French cinema cautions against seeing a copy as a linear derivative of an original and instead argues for the need to acknowledge "circles of intertextuality and hybridity."[13] In other words, a text is linked to what comes before it and what is yet to be created. When we're aware of these related texts, we can access the liminal space between texts and the rich contexts that bear them. From this vantage point, we can analyze these linkages to see not only how a text travels, but how it transforms. This approach also problematizes the notion of an original being the ideal against which other iterations are measured. Furthermore, Mazdon lauds adaptation as cross-cultural interaction and exchange, which should be understood as "a site of difference" instead of as "a site of the same," where "the plurality and contingency of meaning and of textual possibilities should be continuously invoked."[14] Adaptation allows numerous ways of meaning-making, creative expression, and cultural engagement, which are carried across multiple borders.

The rich variety of adaptations of "Ne me quitte pas" proves its mobility and virality. The rest of this chapter will use case studies to explore the diverse and divergent ways "Ne me quitte pas" transgresses and transforms. It will focus on Brazilian bossa nova artist Maysa Matarazzo's rendition of "Ne me quitte pas" in Pedro Almodóvar's *La ley del deseo* (Law of desire), Sasha Velour's drag performance of Bassey's "If You Go Away" at Bizarre in Brooklyn, and Claudio Carneiro's vaudevillian lip-synch of Simone's version for Cirque du Soleil's *Varekai*. These analyses will consider who has the right to a text, to what extent performers appropriate other voices in claiming a text, and how new cultural and social contexts influence the affective experience associated with a text.

Case Studies

Maysa Matarazzo's "Ne me quitte pas" in
La ley del deseo

Pedro Almodóvar's 1987 hit film *La ley del deseo* prominently features Matarazzo's version of "Ne me quitte pas," both as part of the soundtrack and as a plot device.[15] The song first appears twelve minutes in when director Pablo Quintero opens the door of his Madrid apartment to his young lover Juan on the eve of Juan's return to his hometown. As they kiss, Pablo talks about his unrequited love for Juan, before asking Juan to leave to make the separation easier on him. In the background we hear Matarazzo sing the famed line about offering pearls of rain in rainless countries. At that moment, Pablo invites Juan in so they can be together one last time. This offering of the impossible in the lyrics corresponds with Pablo and Juan's success in staving off their separation for a little longer. As they lie in bed caressing each other, Matarazzo sings the song's refrain. Soon after, Juan asks if it's OK if they don't have sex. They embrace as the scene cuts to sunrise over Madrid while Matarazzo sings about the king who died. The scene cuts back to Pablo and Juan asleep, naked in each other's arms, as Matarazzo sings the refrain once more, which is particularly poignant since Juan will indeed leave Pablo soon.

The song returns thirty-nine minutes into the film when Pablo's transgender sister, Tina, plays the female lead in Pablo's new play, an adaptation of Jean Cocteau's one-woman monologue *La voix humaine* (*The Human Voice*). As Tina's character destroys the scene's bedroom with an ax, ten-year-old Ada, the daughter of Tina's absent girlfriend, lip-synchs "Ne me quitte pas" in the foreground stage right. Ada raises her left hand above her head and her right hand to her waist, as if she's looking at a wristwatch when Matarazzo sings about "ces heures" (these hours). The position of her arm, the closed fist, and the red scrunchie give the impression that Ada is stabbing herself in the abdomen when Matarazzo sings, "Tuaient parfois..." (Would sometimes kill...). Suddenly Ada, who is standing on a dolly, rolls to center stage while Matarazzo starts singing the second verse about offering pearls of rain. Ada, embodying Matarazzo's voice, takes up all the space of the scene while Tina collapses on the bed in the background. As soon as the last "ne me quitte pas" of the refrain is mouthed, the phone rings and the music stops. Ada goes offstage to her dressing room and is surprised by her mother, who asks her to move with her to Milan. Ada informs her she will stay with Tina, refusing to abandon her. The camera pans back to Tina, who is still performing her part by speaking on the telephone. Ada returns to the stage and Matarazzo's voice reemerges with "Je ne vais plus pleurer" (I am no longer going to cry). By the end of the song, Ada sings aloud the last refrain over Matarazzo's track and seems to begin crying, perhaps in character, perhaps emotional from her encounter with her mother. A couple of scenes later Ada tells Tina she will never leave her. She then prays at a home-made altar for Pablo to never leave them like her mother did. The song's message thus continues well past the scene.

These two uses of "Ne me quitte pas" show how a song can be adapted to the purposes of a film in various ways. "Ne me quitte pas" serves as Juan's theme in the first scene, which contrasts with the song "Lo dudo" (I doubt it), ostensibly the theme of Antonio, Pablo's other lover and Juan's eventual murderer.[16] In the scene between Pablo and Juan, "Ne me quitte pas" aptly conveys the feeling of impending loss, which augments the dialogue and interactions and thus raises the stakes of their ill-fated relationship. As Almodóvar explicitly notes in an interview with Frédéric Strauss, "Songs play an active part in my films. They're not just decoration, they're a form of dialogue and tell you a lot about the characters."[17] Meanwhile, the second use of "Ne me quitte pas" moves the song from the background to the foreground, transforming it from disembodied film music into a central element of the play. Ada's physical movement to center stage halfway through the song as she embodies Matarazzo's voice highlights the shift in focus. It also expands the theme of abandonment to encompass more than just sexual love. "Ne me quitte pas" thus becomes instrumental in elevating the focus on family, especially chosen family, and the centering of Tina and Ada's storyline about loneliness and loss.

The inclusion of "Ne me quitte pas" in the play scene also offers intriguing cultural and linguistic resonances. Almodóvar explains how he "rendered a kind of unconscious homage to French culture by using Brel's song and Cocteau's *La voix humaine*, two texts which for [him] have the same meaning . . . in terms of abandonment."[18] The choice of language and the slippage between film and stage further highlight the theme of isolation and separation: "With 'Ne me quitte pas' playing, a different language appears to give even more texture to an already textured film. . . . There is a double sensation of foreignness here, and even a kind of double alienation, insisted upon by the foreign text as well as by the fact that the camera is filming a stage."[19] Adaptation, of both a song and an artistic genre, brings the foreign to the fore and allows for multiple vectors of travel in a short period of time.[20]

Moreover, Almodóvar's selection of the singer indicates how foreignness is signified by more than just the French language. It is unknown why Almodóvar did not use Brel. The obvious motive would be that a female voice better aligns with the female protagonist. However, Almodóvar has a penchant for subverting gender conventions and expectations, such as having transgender actress Bibiana Fernández play a cis woman and cisgender actress Carmen Maura play a trans woman in the film. His choice of Matarazzo, who preserves Brel's original lyrics and thus the perspective of a male narrator, suggests a fluid approach to gender. Another reason to choose Matarazzo is that she offers a transatlantic crossing that brings Brazil into the fold: "It will not be the last time that Almodóvar tries to link a particular mode of expression of sensibility to Brazil: Brazilian singer Caetano Veloso sings an extraordinary version of the Mexican classic 'Cucurrucucú Paloma' in *Talk to Her*."[21] The nod to Brazil offers yet another way for "Ne me quitte pas" to travel, morph, and adapt to a new setting. A Brazilian singing in French in a Spanish film crosses multiple linguistic and cultural borders that mirror the boundaries adaptation traverses.

Sasha Velour Performs Bassey at Bizarre

While *La ley del deseo* refers to the stage, Sasha Velour's adaptation of Shirley Bassey's 1967 single "If You Go Away" centers it.[22] In the version performed in April 2017 at the Drag and Brunch Bar Bizarre in Bushwick, Brooklyn, Velour enters the scene in a black knee-length trench coat. Her long, dangling silver earrings accentuate her bald head as she dons a huge smile before mouthing the title line. While lip-synching, she delicately moves her hands, repositioning them slowly in time with each line. Halfway through the first refrain, someone in the audience hands Velour a stack of paintings on paper, the first of which shows a woman in black clutching her chest. When the second verse begins, Velour quickly displays and then tosses away each image one by one. Many of the images are a direct representation of the lyrics. For instance, "We'll sail on the sun, we'll ride on the rain, we'll talk to the trees, and worship the wind" corresponds with a camel-riding caravan in front of a large yellow orb, a boat riding on cresting waves, a couple carving into a tree, and a hot air balloon in flight, respectively. The last painting displays a bald white figure in a bright red dress removing a black coat.

As the third verse commences, Velour undoes her jacket belt, turns her back to the audience, and casts off the garment to reveal a vibrant red long-sleeve dress that matches her stark red lipstick—actions foreshadowed by the parade of images. Unencumbered by the paintings, Velour's body movements become more pronounced. She stretches her arms out farther and mouths the words more prominently. At the beginning of the fourth verse, Velour receives another stack of images, and she resumes displaying and jettisoning them. This time the series depicts a white humanoid figure in a red leotard, garter, and high heels along with a naked pink humanoid figure in a red skullcap. In one image, the white figure, who has pointy ears and fang-like teeth, bites the pink figure's neck as a trickle of blood emerges. In another image, the pink figure seems to escape, leaving the white figure lying on the floor and beckoning for them to return. Velour then sheds her skirt for the final verse, now clad only in the red leotard, garter, and high heels already indicated in the images. The images become more and more abstract until they're reduced to splotches of color. It appears the figure in the red leotard has completely mangled and destroyed the other figure. The final painting is primarily black, with a few tendrils of red seeping from the bottom left corner and two stylized blue eyes with eye shadow, which hint at the shape of Velour's own eyes. As the last image falls to the floor and the music fades, Velour subtly raises her right eyebrow, breaking the trance she held over the audience.

Velour's performance is such a successful adaptation because of how she smoothly marries the visual and the aural through various forms of media to provide the audience with competing and sometimes conflicting narratives. The music is a love song whose speaker makes grandiose promises to stave off abandonment. As discussed in chapter 3, this approach to loss breeds both sadness and hope, a feeling that remains relatively stable throughout the song. Velour's first round of illustrations does similar work since the images on paper align with the images the lyrics convey. Her flowing arm movements and intense eye contact further enhance this complex mix of hopeful sorrow. By the end of the third verse, when she lip-synchs, "I'll be dying slowly until the next hello," her rigid stance embodies a statue frozen in time. Tension resonates through the lyrics, illustrations, and body language.

The fourth verse represents a rupture, the moment the taut string finally snaps. Bassey raises the volume and intensity of her singing, which mirrors the lyrics' pleading nature. While this sonic change stands out to the listener, it's in line with the expectations put forth by the lyrics. What's unexpected is how Velour's body movements become jerky and the illustrations violent, which creates a jarring disconnect with the lyrics' tenderness. Then, in the final verse, the series of paintings implies that Velour's character has ripped her lover to shreds—a grizzly death scene in stark contrast to the defeated, abandoned lover of the song's narrative. Velour's performance thus gives the speaker power in ways the lyrics don't. There's also a certain irony to the words "if you go away" because normally abandonment signals a lack of agency, which isn't the case for Velour's murderous character. The aural and visual elements conflict with and complement each other to elicit a response out from the spectator. Hope mingles with horror in an emotional and sensory roller coaster neither McKuen nor Bassey probably intended.

As with the biographical story of Brel's writing "Ne me quitte pas," the details of this piece's inception imbue Velour's performance with even more emotional heft. Charles Quittner's review of Velour's *Smoke and Mirrors*, another show in which she performs "If You Go Away," provides insight into the performer's life: "Velour had to actually justify monster feminism to their late, scholar mother (a critic of the piece). This version of the number was left unperformed until after she died of cancer. Now, the song takes on a sadder double meaning with lyrics like 'If you go away, as I know you must, there'll be nothing left in this world to trust.'"[23] The performance's impact lands differently when considering Velour's relationship with their mother and decision to shelve this performance in her lifetime.[24] Velour shaving their head as an homage to their mother's struggle with cancer further contextualizes the visuals' thoughtfulness.[25] Meanwhile, the vampiric figure in red, which Quittner refers to as Nosferatess, suggests a move by Velour to question cultural representations of those who violate gender roles and norms, which is a primary aim of drag.[26]

Drag performance is a productive art form for toying with expectations, particularly around understandings of gender. As a site of ambivalence, it uses parody to call attention to the performative nature of gender and the ways it's socially and culturally constructed.[27] Usually, this parody is enacted through lip-synching, though it's important to note that drag didn't always include this practice: "The advent of low-cost high fidelity has led to the technological democratization of the voices of great singers. Almost overnight, mere shower singers became Evelyn Champagne Kings or Shirley Basseys, while true vocal artists were stripped of their unique power to embody the likenesses of those same stars."[28] Just as musical recordings allowed for the invention of an original that could then be covered, easy access to high-quality recordings created a way for anyone to borrow someone's voice and briefly make it their own. The mention of Shirley Bassey specifically demonstrates her central role in the formation of drag culture.

Velour's decision to lip-synch Bassey is not only a parody of gender that allows her to take ownership of a female-identified voice in a general sense; she's also parodying a specific performer and performance. As I watch Velour, I keep thinking about how well the source material lends itself to drag. Velour lip-synchs to Bassey's 1967 single, which points to the importance of this discrete musical track and its musical afterlives. However, Velour has captured and repackaged Bassey's stage presence, which could only have been studied through live performances. Bassey's exaggerated facial expressions, particularly how she moves her lips even when not singing, is a technique Velour employs throughout her lip-synch: "Mouthing each utterance, each breath with astonishing accuracy, exposing aural details that the unaided ear might not catch, suggesting visuals that enlarge and dramatize the vocal performance…make[s] a great vocal performance even greater."[29] Velour's success stems from accomplishing all these feats but also through subtler gestures. For instance, it seems Velour pays homage to Bassey in the first painting, where the figure's black coat and hat look similar to Bassey's outfit and coiffure from the 1976 *Shirley Bassey Show* performance. When the hat falls off in the next painting, showcasing Velour's signature bald head, the sequence suggests Velour emerging from Bassey like a butterfly from a chrysalis.

Velour isn't the first, nor will she be the last, to perform Bassey's music or embody her likeness. An amusing article about Sydney, Australia's Gay and Lesbian Mardi Gras parade recounts how forty-eight Shirley Basseys "in evening dresses, black wigs and boas shimmied along to the beat of *Goldfinger* and *Hey Big Spender*."[30] Meanwhile, Andy Medhurst articulates Bassey's appeal by describing her as "a melodrama in eyelashes and heels, a true queen."[31] What I find most alluring is how Bassey subverts expectations around realness through her self-mockery. However, Bassey not only left her mark on drag but was inspired by it: "Those restless arms, the gestural arabesques which remain her trade-mark, were in fact learned from a queeny choreographer friend, an intriguing example of femininity borrowing from effeminacy, rather than vice versa." It's no wonder Velour built on and adapted Bassey's performances and persona to problematize gender norms and tell her own story about loss and abandonment. Bassey, Velour, and their relationship to drag indicate *trans + latio* and how the act of carrying across can happen in both directions.

Claudio Carneiro Performs Simone in Cirque du Soleil's *Varekai*

Claudio Carneiro, a performer from Brazil, is one of two clowns in *Varekai*, a Cirque du Soleil production that premiered in Montreal in 2002. Carneiro and fellow clown Mooky Cornish offer comedic interludes about every thirty minutes throughout the show. While the acrobatic numbers all appear to be part of a larger story centering around the Greek myth of Icarus, Carneiro and Mooky's performances work outside the narrative arc.

In his performance of Simone's "Ne me quitte pas," Carneiro wears a cyan blue tuxedo with a shiny matching bowtie and cummerbund over a ruffled white shirt.[32] A lone tendril of slicked-back hair forms a black letter *J* on his forehead, and a smear of red blush lines his cheeks. He holds a microphone in his right hand and grasps a golden pole—a stylized tree—with his left. The stage is pitch black except for the spotlight on Carneiro. He begins lip-synching, slowly moving his head as if scanning the audience. Simone's emotion-tinged voice and the pleading melody contrast with Carneiro's colorful ensemble, but the seriousness of his facial expressions and his subtle mouthing of the lyrics capture the song's gravitas.

Near the end of the first verse, the spotlight begins moving without Carneiro. He looks shocked. Trying to follow the light, he bumps into the pole, infusing the performance with the humor one might expect when first seeing his flashy appearance. At this moment, the spotlight transforms into a character in the narrative. Each time Carneiro mouths the title phrase the spotlight slowly moves away and he must catch it to avoid disappearing into the dark abyss, which elicits laugher from the audience. This schtick continues in the second verse.

At the beginning of the third verse, after he pretends to fall down a set of stairs that suddenly appears on stage, Carneiro looks up at the audience, raises and lowers one eyebrow in rapid succession, and winks exaggeratedly with the other eye while opening his mouth wide. His relationship with the spotlight intensifies, as he must run across stage to catch it and even jump to reach it. The spotlight then drags Carneiro into the audience, where he briefly sits on the laps of several patrons as he serenades them. By the end of the fourth verse, the spotlight has multiplied into three. Each one dances around the stage as Carneiro runs among them. When he finally reaches one, his pronounced facial expression suggests annoyance.

As the song transitions to the fifth verse, the spotlight shines on Carneiro, who's now pointing a gun at the rafters, to the audience's delight. He then sheepishly hides the gun behind his back as the applause increases. Suddenly, Carneiro appears to climb one of the golden poles, indicating his intent to reach the source of the spotlight. When he realizes the audience sees him, he sheepishly slides down and starts crawling around on the floor before falling into a hole. In the last refrain, he stands in the hole pointing a small flashlight on his face as he mouths the last lines, then disappears. A spotlight then highlights Mooky up in the rafters, suggesting she is behind the other spotlight's abandonment of Carneiro.

With his "fabulous cabaret deconstruction," Carneiro succeeds in conveying humor by parodying the genre of chanson in ways that defy our expectations.[33] Óscar Quezada-Macchiavello underscores Carneiro's use of burlesque imitation to mock the seriousness associated with certain chanson ballads.[34] In particular, Carneiro plays with established lighting conventions, highlighting the taken-for-granted relationship between performer and stage crew as well as the reliance solo performers have on the spotlight. This disruption of the spectator's expectation precipitates the spotlight's ability to transform into Carneiro's coactor. The spotlight's personification also affects the listener's interpretation of the lyrics, where the *you* no longer refers to the listener but to an inanimate object, creating emotional distance between the singer and the audience. At the same time, this distance makes it easier for the audience to find humor in a song about despair and abandonment.

Although Carneiro's incorporation of the refrain is obvious—he tries to stay in a spotlight that repeatedly abandons him with each "ne me quitte pas"—his interaction with the rest of the lyrics is less convincing. Quezada-Macchiavello's close reading of the performance implies subtle connections between the lyrics and Carneiro's actions, but I find it hard to connect the physicality of his performance with the words.[35] The only time I really sense a link between the two is when Carneiro falls to the floor during "l'ombre de ta main, l'ombre de ton chien" (shadow of your hand, shadow of your dog) and crawls on his hands and knees like a dog in the dark. Regardless, I think Carneiro's skit is highly effective precisely because of the disconnect between his humorous performance and the sadness conveyed through the lyrics and music. He captures the notion that tears and anguish are often the driving force behind comedy.

Adapting Realness

While all three case studies revolve around lip-synched versions of "Ne me quitte pas," they yield very different viewing experiences. As a clown, Carneiro's intention is primarily comedic, and the audience's exuberant laughter registers his success. He remarks in an interview "what a joy it is to inspire audiences to have fun night after night" and explains how the most rewarding part of his job is "to hear the audience's laughter."[36] Meanwhile, Velour's use of dark humor seems to achieve more difficult goals as she works to challenge societal conceptualizations of gender and create space for personal reflection on loss. The audience's hollers suggest empowerment and transmit uplifting energy in the face of horror. As for Almodóvar's use of "Ne me quitte pas," there are no audience reactions to provide a sense of how viewers respond. Even if I had experienced the film in theaters, there probably wouldn't have been any noticeable outwardly directed reaction from the audience, as films tend to elicit less audience participation than staged acts. However, I'm personally moved by and appreciate the multiple layers and perspectives achieved at this moment. There's the scene on stage that tells the characters' story, the scene backstage that tells a different story about the actors' lives, and the film's narrative, with its critiques of family, gender, and love. The lip-synching, just like these nested stories, serves to remind us of the porous boundaries between art and life.

These three performances also diverge in how the elements of violence land. The violence in *La ley del deseo* is both understated and palpable. Ada's character barely moves as Tina's ax-wielding character destroys the background. I find Tina's grunts, which disrupt the sonic beauty of Matarazzo's voice, more violent than her overacted visual destruction. My mind wanders as it looks for symbolism, such as when I notice the red scrunchie's gesture to blood. I therefore experience violence on a more intellectual level than a visceral one. Meanwhile, Carneiro's tumble down the stairs and fall into the hole verge on slapstick. It's even hard to take Carneiro's prop pistol seriously because he's threating an inanimate object. Much like when watching cartoon violence (e.g., the misadventures of *Looney Tunes*' Wile E. Coyote), the spectator doesn't really feel sadness or sympathy for the victim. As for Velour, while her outlandish cartoon images of a brutal and bloody attack run the risk of desensitizing the horror they evoke, she creatively marries the substance of the lyrics with the visual imagery. Because of Velour's convincing embodiment of sorrowful abandonment, the spectator becomes more invested in the outcome and feels the violence more deeply.

I gravitate most to thoughts about authenticity and embodiment, particularly in the cases of Carneiro and Velour, where white performers lip-synch Black women. It's unclear whether Carneiro's choice of music has any deeper meaning than the aesthetic value Simone brings. I've yet to find any interviews with Carneiro or the Cirque du Soleil team that mention this number's conception, and I've already argued that there's nothing about the performance that clearly connects it to this particular recording. Because *Varekai* originated in Montreal—a francophone North American city—there's a tepid connection to fellow North American entertainer Simone and a possible desire to acknowledge the French language (though the latter could've been done by lip-synching Brel). Regardless of the reasons for its inclusion, using a recorded song is notable because the rest of the show appears to rely on live musicians performing original music. While lip-synching Simone could suggest paying homage to a great performer, it also follows a long tradition of co-opting Black voices.

Meanwhile, as mentioned above, Shirley Bassey's over-the-top performances lend themselves to drag. But Medhurst's comments on Bassey's lack of mainstream femininity hint at a long-standing discourse around Black women's inability to claim a type of femininity that has always been associated with whiteness.[37] Since gender-bending performance relies on challenging expectations, and race plays an important role in cultural expectations, white performers' embodiment of Black voices aren't neutral acts. Moreover, as E. Patrick Johnson shows, understandings of queer theory and performance usually don't consider the material realities, subjectivities, and agency of racially minoritized people.[38] Elsewhere, Johnson argues that "when white-identified subjects perform 'black' signifiers—normative or otherwise—the effect is always already entangled in the discourse of otherness; the historical weight of white skin privilege necessarily engenders a tense relationship with its Others."[39] He then demonstrates how language use is one of the most common ways to appropriate Blackness. While discussions of appropriation may focus on the use of certain sociolects associated with Black speakers, such as African American English, these two cases of lip-synching of Black women's actual voices mark an even more extreme form of appropriation.

Concluding Thoughts

This rumination on appropriation allows us to return to the discussion of real voice, which exudes, among other things, emotional truthfulness and authenticity.[40] *Jacques Brel Is Alive and Well* and *La ley del deseo* show how situating a song in a larger narrative influences our readings of real voice. One may assume Brel singing his own song—which, in chapter 1, I contend is very convincing in conveying a real voice—would create favorable conditions for this real voice to reemerge. Indeed, Brel comes across as sincere, but the film is so strange that his voice loses some of its realness in that context. A poorly executed adaptation has thus stripped away the affective dimension, the emotional truthfulness, of his performance. The real voice becomes even more muddled in *La ley del deseo* because of the many layers of adaptation seen through a Spanish child actress lip-synching a Brazilian woman's cover of a Belgian man's song in a staging of a French monologue for a Spanish film. However, the play's interruption—the brief arrival of the absentee mother, which solidifies the theme of abandonment—provides an emotional gut punch that helps bring a real voice to the surface.

The two stage productions demonstrate yet another perspective on adaptation. Velour takes Bassey's rendition of "If You Go Away"—which is the least "real" among Brel's, Simone's, and Bassey's—and injects realness through the sheer intensity of her performance. One would think a theatrical drag performance of theatrical source material would further distance the spectator and thereby dilute realness, but this act has the most emotional resonance of the adaptations, in my opinion. However, not knowing the backstory about Velour's mother might make their voice feel less real because the biographical information has implications for our viewing experience. The politics of transgressing racial boundaries and what this means for authenticity further calls into question any claims on realness. And finally, I find that the disconnect between the silly humor of Carneiro's performance and the overwhelming realness of Simone's voice creates the largest distance to realness among the four adaptations. The act's racial crossing also adds to this rupture, especially since nothing in the performance taps into the emotions Simone lays bare, emotions that capture the weight of the traumatic racialized Othering Simone endured throughout her life. Carneiro's performance serves as an interlude disconnected from the rest of *Varekai*, further minimizing Simone's affective power. At the same time, Carneiro traffics in humor and convincingly builds an emotional connection through laughter. As such, his adaptation is a success.

Regardless of how well each case study achieves a real voice and to what extent the processes of adaptation alter the affective qualities of Brel's, Simone's, and Bassey's "originals," the performances analyzed in this chapter all succeed in multiple forms of boundary-crossing. They show the diversity and prevalence of adaptations and all the different ways art moves us. The various performances also highlight the importance of singles and how crucial these iconic recorded versions are to artistic genres that rely on lip-synching. Furthermore, the examples in this chapter remind us how adaptations can be untethered from the source text to the point where we can't even find the original, which suggests that in *trans + latio*, once something is carried across, it's possible for that link to be severed. It makes me wonder what else in my life is an adaptation? And does it matter if I never trace it back?

Outro

THE EARWORM HAS BEEN WITH ME all evening. *Da-da-da-da-daaa*. Sometimes it's just rhythm, and my foot taps along. Sometimes it's a series of notes tickling the back of my throat. English may peek its head out but usually makes way for French. Often Nina's voice will summon me, her piano keys whisking me away. Other times, visions of Brel's dripping sweat seem to stain my mind's eye before Velour's Nosferatess claws its way into view. Bassey looks on, statuesque and stately. A kaleidoscope of images, sounds, emotions, and memories refracted from one single song.

Through "Ne me quitte pas," a text transforms, travels, and thrives in multiple settings. Covering imbues the song with altered meanings, from the stylistic choices a performer makes to its interactions with the new audiences it reaches. Translation takes the song in other directions by exposing it to new linguistic structures and cultural traditions. Adaptation enables the song to travel across genres and media. And while some lament what gets lost in these various transformations, I like to focus on what is gained.

I set out to tell the story of a single song. Instead I uncovered its multiplicity and instability. And as I've tried to understand my relationship with this song, I've wound up awed by its many connections with diverse audiences. A song isn't just text and sound. It's a set of lived, performed audiovisual experiences influenced by a range of contexts and media—in studio, on stage, on screen, and online. And we can measure its success based on the transcendence of the emotional reactions it triggers and the impact of these affective elements on our individual and collective experiences.

While I have spent the whole book arguing that a song's power resides in how it affects its creator and its listener, we must not reduce a song to an artifact of its creation, performance, and reception. It exists as something outside any particular author, performer, or listener. What a song does is integral to the song itself. The generic category of a single signifies border-crossing and mobility not because of what it is, but because of the potential it holds. Brel's original recording was the catalyst for this song's incredible journey, and we have yet to see where it ends.

Witnessing how this song travels has taught me about what it means to be human. Simone's cover showed me early on that Black women can speak and sing in French when everything around me suggested otherwise. In a way, she expands the definition of francophone in a way that is not just tied to ability. It's her desire to perform and inhabit the French language that strengthens her claim to francophone identity. Furthermore, her stories about "Ne me quitte pas" demonstrate the nuances of a lived Black experience and how it intersects with language and nation. Meanwhile, Bassey's rendition of "If You Go Away" doesn't have the same racial subtext, but perhaps there's a connection to the mask she seems to wear throughout her performance. Carneiro's and Velour's lip-synching performances turn my attention to appropriation and the act of Black voices leaving white mouths. Do I react to the racial dimension of Velour's performance less viscerally because Bassey herself was so good at playing a role in this song? Or is it because Velour uses the source material more convincingly to tell their own deeply personal story? This is the beauty of all these iterations: they get me to think and feel so deeply.

Even songs that haven't traveled as extensively through covers, translations, and adaptations offer multiplicity and instability. We think of songs as having lineages—a linear movement through time from the original to the copy, from the single to the multiple. But any singer can claim ownership, argue authenticity, and decide whether to channel a real voice, regardless of who sang it first. It's for the public to judge. Furthermore, all songs drum up images and emotions attached to sounds and words, and this bursting kaleidoscope of sensations doesn't have a discernable beginning or end. That's the power of song. It might send me to the past when I hop on a memory or send me to the future when it beckons me to dream big. And, at the same time, I'm present in the music, in touch with my emotions. I can simultaneously be everywhere at all times.

ACKNOWLEDGMENTS

I am so grateful to all the people who made my research pivot into music studies possible. I am indebted to the Popular Music Books in Process series that put Singles on my radar and to series editors Joshua Clover and Emily Lordi who encouraged me to propose this book. Many thanks to Ken Wissoker who was always so thoughtful in helping me navigate the review process. I am also extremely appreciative of the three anonymous reviewers who provided such generous, astute, and thought-provoking feedback.

I express my gratitude to the University of Washington, whose Research Royalty Fund and Society of Scholars gave me the funding and time needed to research and write this book. The observations that my fellow colleagues in Society of Scholars shared for an early draft of chapter 2 set the tone for the whole book. Similarly, I thoroughly enjoyed the music department's discussion of my book manuscript near the end of the writing process. Their comments helped solidify various arguments. I commend the students in my Francophone music course for engaging with the various versions of "Ne me quitte pas" and offering excellent analyses. I'm also grateful to colleagues who provided substantive feedback, including L. J. Müller, Richard Watts, Olivia Gunn, and Gabriel Solis.

Thanks to Noah Lubert, my instructor for my songwriting certificate from Berklee College of Music, who added to my musical foundation and looked over my musical analyses. Shout-out to my research assistant Sandra Bonequi, who sifted through hundreds of articles and books to point me toward relevant passages. Much respect to Anitra Budd, who made my musings more accessible to a wider audience. I also appreciate the numerous interlocutors I've crossed paths with over the past couple of years who listened to me excitedly talk about this project. The insights they shared took this book to places I couldn't have imagined when I first started on this path. For instance, I thank Maxine Savage for introducing me to Sasha Velour's drag performance of "If You Go Away."

I am indebted to my wonderful family whose unwavering support has made me the writer that I am. Rohit, Amar'e, Emily, Elton, Jonathan, Stephanie, Mathew, Susan, Rajiv, Archana, and everyone else, I thank you from the bottom of my heart. Finally, I want to honor Nina Simone. This book is an homage to her for the guidance her music has offered throughout my life.

NOTES

Chapter 1. "Ne me quitte pas": Jacques Brel Composes the Ultimate Breakup Song

1. Jacques Brel, "'Ne me quitte pas,'" *Palmarès des chansons*, 1966, INA, https://www.ina.fr/ina-eclaire-actu/video/i07046439/jacques-brel-ne-me-quitte-pas.

2. Looseley, *Popular Music*, 68; Poole, *Brel and Chanson*, xv.

3. Blau and Brel, *Jacques Brel Is Alive and Well*, 35. See Gorin, "Jacques Brel," 234, for a discussion of Brel's prêtre-ouvrier identity.

4. Hawkins, *Chanson*, 59.

5. Hawkins, *Chanson*, 63.

6. François Gorin referred to Brel's father Romain as "un Flamand francophone, traître à la cause 'flamingande'" (a French-speaking Fleming, traitor to the "Flemish" cause). Gorin, "Jacques Brel," 221. This suggestion of cultural treason indicates the complex nature of Belgian identity while also emphasizing the importance of the French language to Brel's family. Interestingly, Marc Robine noted how Brel struggled in his Flemish courses (*Grand Jacques*, 35).

7. Haworth, "Singer-Songwriter on Stage," 78; Poole, *Brel and Chanson*, xv. See also Haworth, "French *Chanson*."

8. Gorin, "Jacques Brel," 224–25.

9. Berruer, *Jacques Brel va bien*, 61.

10. The state's role in promoting art and culture predates the Ministry of Culture by centuries with state-sponsored museums, such as the Louvre, and arbiters of language and culture, such as members of the Académie Française.

11. Rigaud, *L'exception culturelle*, 50.

12. Hare, "Popular Music on French Radio and Television," 58.

13. After twenty-eight years of French television, a second state-run channel was added in 1964. See Hare, "Popular Music on French Radio and Television"; and Tinker, "One State, One Television, One Public."

14. Hare, "Popular Music on French Radio and Television."

15. Loisy, "Avant-propos," 7.

16. Loisy, "Ne me quitte pas," 39.

17. Cohn, *Distinction of Fiction*, 112.

18. Gorin, "Jacques Brel," 234.

19. Loisy, "Ne me quitte pas," 40. The more dramatic version of this story claims that Gabriello was pregnant and left Brel when he refused to acknowledge paternity of their unborn child, leading her to get an abortion. This version has not been corroborated.

20. Loisy, "Avant-propos," 11.

21. Loisy, "Ne me quitte pas," 41. See also Vincendet, *Jacques Brel, l'impossible rêve*, 188.

22. Duponchelle, *"Ne me quitte pas* de Jacques Brel." See also Vincendet, *Jacques Brel, l'impossible rêve*, 76.

23. Cordier, "Chanson and Tacit Misogyny," 39, 41. See also Bibard, *Penser avec Brel*. Brel, at points in his life, even saw himself as a misogynist, although this self-assessment fluctuates. See Cristiani and Leloir, *Trois hommes dans un salon*, 65–66.

24. Hawkins, *Chanson*, 39.

25. Tinker, *George Brassens and Jacques Brel*, 2. See also Yacobi, "Package Deals in Fictional Narrative."

26. Tinker, *George Brassens and Jacques Brel*, 2.

27. Hongre and Lidsky, *Jacques Brel*, 5.

28. Riggan, *Pícaros, Madmen, Naïfs, and Clowns*, 20.

29. Loisy, "Ne me quitte pas," 39–40; Vincendet, *Jacques Brel, l'impossible rêve*, 74–75.

30. Occasionally there are lines that could be read as either four or six syllables, depending on pronunciation or elision of vowels.

31. Because of their poetic nature, Brel's lyrics are notoriously difficult to translate, especially when considering excerpts that don't convey the full meaning. My translations barely scratch the surface of possible meanings.

32. I'm interested in Brel as both a songwriter and a performer. This section will consider what he wrote in the sheet music as well as what he does in the aforementioned performance.

33. Robine, *Grand Jacques*, 166.

34. Hawkins, *Chanson*, 53.

35. Hawkins, *Chanson*, 144.

36. Interestingly, the sheet music shows an E^7 chord instead of a C.

37. Hawkins, *Chanson*, 146. See also Monestier, *Brel*, 16, who provided the translation.

38. Cordier, "Chanson and Tacit Misogyny," 46.

39. Blau and Brel, *Jacques Brel Is Alive and Well*, 20.

40. Müller, *Hearing Sexism*, 44. I will address the racial aspect of Müller's argument, the "hegemonic White male concept of the body," when discussing Nina Simone's cover.

41. Hongre and Lidsky argue that the Brelian hero is crushed because he cannot seduce and begs for tenderness because he is unable to impose his desire as a man (*Jacques Brel*, 28).

42. Vincendet, *Jacques Brel, l'impossible rêve*, 76.

43. I base this reading on an argument L. J. Müller makes in their analysis of Birdy's performance of "People Help the People" (*Hearing Sexism*, 166).

44. See Charpentreau and Charpentreau, *La chanson*, for more on authenticity.

45. Angela Davis highlights the connection of mind and body when she writes, "Art is special because of its ability to influence feelings as well as knowledge" (*Blues Legacies and Black Feminism*, xiii).

46. Ahmed, *Queer Phenomenology*, 2.

47. Ahmed, *Queer Phenomenology*, 2.

48. Ahmed, *Cultural Politics of Emotion*, 8.

49. Interestingly, Brel thought of this moment as a singular event. A week after the event, Charley Marouani sent a letter to M. Jolivand reminding him that Brel's contract stipulated this episode could only air live that one night. No other airings were allowed. A copy of this letter can be found in the archive of the Institut National de l'Audiovisuel (ina).

50. Jacques Brel, "'Ne me quitte pas' (live official)," YouTube, uploaded by INA Chansons, July 9, 2012, https://youtu.be/n0ehZeWGXW0?.

Chapter 2. "Sorry about the Words, Y'all": Nina Simone Covers Brel

1. Thierry Ardisson, "Nina Simone parle de Jacques Brel," *Bains de minuit*, June 10, 1988, INA, https://www.ina.fr/ina-eclaire-actu/video/i08086104/nina-simone-a-propos-de-jacques-brel.

2. "Read Mary J. Blige's Heartfelt Nina Simone Rock Hall Induction Speech."

3. See Navas, "Originality of Copies"; and Gunkel, *Of Remixology*, for research on covering, including a discussion about values placed on notions of original and copy. Jordan Stein argues that "the strength of the cover … is the extent to which it can upend the who-came-first hierarchy." He suggests that Simone was more interested in being

definitive than original. Stein, *Fantasies of Nina Simone*, 83, 81.

4. According to Navas, covers exist "to reach a wider commercial market, often by adapting the original to the tastes of a new or somewhat different audience" ("Originality of Copies," 169).

5. The debates around whether Beyoncé's album *Cowboy Carter* (Columbia, 2024) and her song "Daddy Lessons" from the album *Lemonade* (Columbia, 2016) should be considered country music demonstrate the difficulty for Black performers to claim a stake in perceived white genres.

6. Weisbard, *Hound Dog*, 36.

7. Cortés, *Little Richard*, 00:19:25.

8. Brelitude, accessed February 28, 2024, http://www.brelitude.net/.

9. The next most popular song is "La chanson des vieux amants" with 693. The website includes covers and translations.

10. Aznavour wrote the music to both songs and the lyrics to the latter, while Yves Stéphane penned the lyrics to the former. Marcel Stellman translated both songs into English. Brun-Lambert, *Nina Simone*, 154.

11. Simone seldom sang anything in a language other than English. However, in 1982, almost two decades after *I Put a Spell on You*, she recorded the album *Fodder on My Wings*, which included some songs either entirely in French or in French and English.

12. Jordan Stein sums up her power: "Listening to Simone cover a song, you never doubt that it is, in every sense, hers." Stein, *Fantasies of Nina Simone*, 76.

13. Cohodas, *Princess Noire*, 164.

14. Feldstein "'I Don't Trust You Anymore,'" 1358. Simone borrowed her last name from the French actress Simone Signoret. Simone and Cleary, *I Put a Spell on You*, 49.

15. Brun-Lambert, *Nina Simone*, 154–55.

16. The change from *quitte* to *quittez* in the title denotes a move from the singular to the plural *you*, where the *you* now refers to Simone's fans and the readers of the book. Brun-Lambert, *Nina Simone*, 324, mentions that a misinformed journalist reported Simone having a nervous breakdown when hearing the new title name, a story translator Mimi Perrin and the publishing house deny.

17. Brooks, "Nina Simone's Triple Play," 179.

18. Brooks, "Nina Simone's Triple Play," 179.

19. Brooks, "Nina Simone's Triple Play," 177.

20. Brooks, "Nina Simone's Triple Play," 177.

21. Brooks, "Nina Simone's Triple Play," 176. Jordan Stein reads this defiance of musical genre as a way for Simone to express "her commitments to opacity—to a fantasy of not

being, or not having to be, wholly legible." Stein, *Fantasies of Nina Simone*, 167.

22. See Stovall, *Paris Noir*, for a detailed history of African Americans in twentieth-century Paris. See also Mitchell, *Vénus Noire*.

23. Nina Simone, "Ne me quitte pas," YouTube, uploaded by Okiedogg, August 22, 2009, https://youtu.be/0Q7w7gk1JhQ?.

24. The sheet music includes these feminized lyrics in parentheses, suggesting that Brel planned for the possibility of different narrative perspectives. Brel, *Ne me quitte pas*, 5. Simone Langlois, "Ne me quitte pas," YouTube, uploaded by Cherry Red Records, May 21, 2022, https://www.youtube.com /watch?v=nnn9eGjRoTI.

25. Barbara, "Ne me quitte pas," YouTube, uploaded by Manuel Rodrigues Lx, June 4, 2017, https://youtu.be/-Upzso5vghM?. In one live version of the song, which is unfortunately not labeled with a date but which seems more recent than the other version, Simone plays with gender. Instead of "Tu seras reine" she sings, "Je seras reine." It suggests an attempt to change the pronoun to reflect that she is the queen here, but she still uses the second person singular verb (i.e., I are queen). While not standard French, it shows that she's thinking about gender and what it means to embody the narration. Nina Simone, "Ne me quitte pas,"

YouTube, uploaded by Santi Pages, March 23, 2008, https://youtu.be/TI8F6DbB2cE?.

26. Describing Simone as bisexual, Salamishah Tillet writes, "Simone's androgynous voice, genre-breaking musicianship and political consciousness . . . are a huge draw for today's gay, lesbian, black and female artists who want to be taken seriously for their talent, their activism or a combination of both" ("Nina Simone's Time is Now, Again"). Alan Light contends that Simone identified as straight, even though at one point she had sex with and loved a woman (*What Happened, Nina Simone?*, 177). Marie-Christine Dunham Pratt reflects on her fleeting love story with Simone in Jeff Lieberman's documentary *The Amazing Nina Simone*. Meanwhile, Jordan Stein warns that "nearly the entire biographical account of Simone's sexuality is based on her ex-husband's speculative report of what she may have done with other people." Stein, *Fantasies of Nina Simone*, 107.

27. Nina Simone, "Ne me quitte pas," *A la manière*, December 18, 1971, ina, https:// www.ina.fr/ina-eclaire-actu/video /i18108504/nina-simone-chante-ne-me -quitte-pas.

28. This vulnerability is also transmitted in the album version when occasionally Simone repeats the title phrase without instrumental support.

29. Jordan Stein argues that Simone's propensity for elongated notes gives her "vocal performances a tension that doesn't really resolve so much as it wears out, adding a richly dejected feel." Stein, *Fantasies of Nina Simone*, 77.

30. Showing how musicians from the African diaspora upend Western conventions, Portia Maultsby argues that they "bring intensity to their performance by alternating lyrical, percussive, and raspy timbres; juxtaposing vocal and instrumental textures; changing pitch and dynamic levels' alternating straight and vibrato tones; and weaving moans, shouts, grunts, hollers, and screams into the melody" ("Africanisms in African-American Music," 191–92).

31. Ardisson, "Nina Simone parle de Jacques Brel."

32. Brun-Lambert, *Nina Simone*, 154.

33. Simone, "Ne me quitte pas," YouTube, uploaded by Okiedogg.

34. In addition to appearing in the INA archive, the 1971 live version was posted on January 23, 2013, on what appears to be Nina Simone's official YouTube channel, run by the Estate and Charitable Trust of Nina Simone: https://youtu.be/GT8slx IPB9g?. This clip contains two songs, "Ne me quitte pas" followed by "My Way," the English-language version of the French song "Comme d'habitude."

35. See Stein, *Fantasies of Nina Simone*, 147–76, for insight on Simone's interactions with audiences.

36. Posner, *Linguistic Change in French*, 11.

37. Benaglia and Smith, "Multilingual Texts and Contexts," 20, argue, "France is probably the modern nation that historically, and even today, has most insisted on the relationship between nationhood and linguistic norm and that has focused its attention on notions such as linguistic purity, standard language, and neutral accent . . . "

38. Since some don't consider the Parisian accent neutral, it holds a lot of cachet. In the same interview Brel talks about finding various French accents charming. "De l'accent bruxellois," YouTube, uploaded by Fondation Jacques Brel, July 19, 2016, https://youtu.be/sWdO9Dop1YE?.

39. One can hear Simone speak a bit of French on April 26, 1967, when Michel Drucker, the host of the variety show *Tilt Magazine*, introduces Simone. Drucker first speaks to Simone in French before translating into nonstandard English: "We are very pleased to see you tonight because in France everybody like you." Simone responds in French, "Je suis—j'ai très heureuse de chanter ce soir dans *Tilt Magazine*" (I am—I have very happy to sing tonight for *Tilt Magazine*). Drucker helps Simone construct this sentence and then remarks,

"C'est très bien" (It's very good). Simone then smiles as she receives applause while walking to the piano to play "Real, Real" and "Ne me quitte pas." The Official Home of Nina Simone, accessed April 19, 2024, https://www.ninasimone.com/1960–1969 /legacy-1967/.

40. Smith, *Senegal Abroad*, 92.

41. Simone, "Ne me quitte pas," YouTube, uploaded by Okiedogg.

42. "Best of Nina Simone."

43. See Gillett, *At Home in Our Sounds*, 6–7.

44. See Stein, *Fantasies of Nina Simone*, 149–50.

45. Simone and Cleary, *I Put a Spell on You*, 69. Until she found a larger purpose with protest music, Simone saw popular music as inferior: "I put as much of my classical background as I could into the songs I performed and the music I recorded, to give it at least some depth and quality" (91).

46. Smitherman, *Talkin and Testifyin*, 48.

47. Neal, *What the Music Said*, 2.

48. Brooks, *Liner Notes for the Revolution*, 3. See also McKittrick, *Dear Science*.

49. However, Simone had a history of inserting politics and protest into unlikely songs. Jordan Stein recounts Simone's first European tour: "She introduces 'Tomorrow Is My Turn,' an English adaptation of Charles Aznavour's love song 'L'amour, c'est comme un jour,' by telling her Dutch audience that when she sings it, 'I make it a protest song.'" Stein, *Fantasies of Nina Simone*, 87. See also Peck, Galloway, and Gulotta, *Nina Simone: Live in '65 and '68*.

50. "Mississippi Goddam" debuted on *Nina Simone in Concert*, her first album since changing to Dutch record label Phillips. Moving to a European-based company made it easier to record protest music critical of the United States. A *Jet* article from March 24, 1986, reports that "she was so torn by her emotions in the freedom struggle that she sent herself into self-imposed exile in Europe and Africa in 1974." As Bettina Judd notes in her analysis of rage in "Mississippi Goddam," "Her incendiary language was met with more ire in the white run music industry than the murder of Medgar Evers itself" (*Feelin*, 164).

51. As Ronald Radano argues, Black voice "can be understood in two ways: as the literal, audible utterance empowering the singing or speaking subject and as a metonym referring to the broad, social impact of a highly racialized African-American performative tradition" (*Lying Up a Nation*, 15). Similarly, Lindon Barrett maintains "the impossibility of divorcing the singing voice from the existence and condition of African Americans in the New World landscape" (*Blackness and Value*, 60).

52. Müller, *Hearing Sexism*, 165–66.

53. Stein, Fantasies of Nina Simone, 57.

54. Müller, *Hearing Sexism*, 169.

55. Brand, *Bread out of Stone*, 161.

56. Judd, *Feelin*, 11–12.

57. For recent research on how the embodied practice of sound production shapes listening experience, see Giomi, "Case for an Embodied Approach." An example would be how a pianist listens differently to a piano than does a person who has never played or even seen someone play a piano.

58. For scholarship on the consumption of Black pain, see Alexander, "'Can You Be Black and Look at This?'"; Wood, *Lynching and Spectacle*; and Frankowski, "Spectacle Terror Lynching."

59. Ardisson, "Nina Simone parle de Jacques Brel."

60. Simone and Cleary, *I Put a Spell on You*, 165.

61. Ardisson, "Nina Simone parle de Jacques Brel." Simone performed "Ne me quitte pas" in Africa as during her 1969 concert at PANAF, the Pan-African Festival of Algiers. See Tolan-Szkilnik, *Maghreb Noir*, 177.

62. Muñoz, *Sense of Brown*, 3.

63. Simone and Cleary, *I Put a Spell on You*, 165.

64. Feldstein, "'I Don't Trust You Anymore,'" 1358.

65. Simone and Cleary, *I Put a Spell on You*, 167.

66. Ardisson, "Nina Simone parle de Jacques Brel."

67. Borawski, "For the Love of Nina," 44. Almost in response, Jacques Brel's "Ne me quitte pas" opened Simone's funeral service. See Light, *What Happened, Miss Simone*, 260.

68. *Nina Revisited . . . A Tribute to Nina Simone* (RCA Records, 2015); Lauryn Hill and the Roots, "Ne Me Quitte Pas (Nina Simone Tribute)," YouTube, uploaded by Rock and Roll Hall of Fame, May 11, 2020, https://youtu.be/UjLcjB478Aw?. Meshell Ndegeocello also has a tribute album to Nina Simone, *Pour une Âme Souveraine: A Dedication to Nina Simone* (Naïve, 2012), which covers some of Simone's greatest hits. Curiously, even though the album has a French title, "Ne me quitte pas" is not included.

Chapter 3. "We'll Sail on the Sun": Rod McKuen and Shirley Bassey Translate Hope in a Song about Despair

1. Interestingly, the esteemed French singer-songwriter Charles Aznavour was a guest on the first episode.

2. Shirley Bassey, "If You Go Away," YouTube, uploaded by kidm2m, July 26, 2008, https://youtu.be/pwGUqx6vngY?.

3. Tinker, "Jacques Brel Is Alive and Well," 180.

4. "Although Brel gave relatively few concerts in the English-speaking world (at the Albert Hall in London in 1966 and at New York's Carnegie Hall in 1965 and 1967), he went on to become one of the most covered French-speaking artists in the USA and in the UK" (Tinker, "Jacques Brel Is Alive and Well," 180).

5. Cordier, *Post-war French Popular Music*, 140. See also *Chorus*, 80.

6. Robine, *Grand Jacques*, 164.

7. Venuti, "Adaptation, Translation, Critique," 30.

8. Lawrence, "Eurovision." For the quote, see Tinker "Jacques Brel Is Alive and Well," 182. I have been unable to find the original.

9. Scott, *German Operetta*, 55.

10. Bassnett, *Translation Studies*, 38. For a detailed discussion of loss in translation, see Venuti, "Adaptation, Translation, Critique," 29.

11. Venuti, "Translation, Community, Utopia," 466.

12. Bassnett, *Translation Studies*, 6.

13. Bassnett, *Translation Studies*, 6, 9–10.

14. For the sake of this discussion, I will not consider literal translations, which "add a level of semantic comprehension, in order to allow the listener to enjoy the original experience of the song on all other levels, musically, theatrically or visually" (Desblache, *Music and Translation*, 219). While these are important interventions (and much more prevalent and accessible than they were when "Ne me quitte pas" was written thanks to the internet), they fall outside the scope of this chapter.

15. Henry Drinker and Andrew Kelly call on translators to "preserve the notes, rhythm, and phrasing of the music" and "respect the rhythms," respectively (Drinker, "On Translating Vocal Texts," 226; Kelly, "Translating French Song," 92).

16. Drinker and Kelly place preserving rhyme near the bottom of their lists. Not all musical traditions rhyme. For a discussion of rhyming and nonrhyming musical traditions, see Low, "Translating Songs That Rhyme."

17. Drinker ranks preserving meaning last in his requirements, while Kelly ranks it second.

18. Low, "Translating Songs That Rhyme," 5.

19. See Venuti, *Translator's Invisibility*, for a discussion on domestication and foreignization.

20. Schudel, "Rod McKuen."

21. Schudel, "Rod McKuen."

22. Tinker, "Jacques Brel Is Alive and Well," 182.

23. Schudel, "Rod McKuen."

24. "Flight Plan for 16 October 2002," Rod McKuen: A Safe Place to Land, last modified June 7, 2015, https://web.archive.org/web/20031122193317/http://rodmckuen.com/flights/161002.htm.

25. According to Schudel, McKuen never understood all the negative criticism: "Before he became well known, Mr. McKuen said, his books usually received laudatory reviews. Only after he became famous, and his music and words sold in the millions, did the reviews turn more critical and even nasty" ("Rod McKuen").

26. Venuti, *Translator's Invisibility*.

27. M. D., "Shirley Bassey Is a Sensation."

28. Bassey, "If You Go Away," YouTube, uploaded by kidm2m.

29. Bassey, *My Life*, 76.

30. "Programme Reviews."

31. Toy, "Shirley Bassey Show."

32. Toy, "Shirley Bassey Show."

33. D. E. H., "Shirley Bassey Is Tops."

34. "Shirley Bassey."

35. Stan, "Shirley Bassey Show."

36. Stan, "Shirley Bassey Show."

37. James, "Resting in Gardens," 2.

38. For a detailed discussion of the effects of animalistic and mechanistic dehumanization on perceptions of women, see Morris, Goldenberg, and Boyd, "Women as Animals."

39. For this analysis, I'm using the lyrics and music found in the sheet music of Brel's album *Ne me quitte pas*.

40. Tinker, "Jacques Brel Is Alive and Well," 184.

41. As Peter Hawkins argues, "One of the characteristics of the French *chanson* tradition is the foregrounding of the lyrics, which are often interpreted in the manner of a dramatic monologue accompanied by music. This is much less the case with Anglo-American popular music, where the tune is all-important" (*Chanson*, 54).

42. While absent in the sheet music, Bassey adds the preposition "on" before "the sun" in the performance analyzed in this chapter. Brel, *Ne me quitte pas*.

43. In the 1967 studio version, Bassey retains the *I* statements McKuen had written but includes "the shadow of your dog," which is a departure from McKuen's original lyrics.

44. Müller, *Hearing Sexism*, 131.

45. Müller, *Hearing Sexism*, 132.

46. "Shirley Bassey."

47. "Possibly, she says, this was because everyone knew that if you called the Bassey children names 'you'd get a punch in the nose'" (Ross, "Sharp as a Diamond"). Bassey's hometown of Tiger Bay, Cardiff, has a long history of multiculturalism dating back to the nineteenth century, attracting sailors and dock workers from across the world. For a detailed discussion of race and migration in Tiger Bay, see Ramdin, *Reimagining Britain*.

48. Medhurst, "Arts." Her biographer, John L. Williams, adds that in *Hot from Harlem* "she and a troupe of other mixed-race Cardiff girls were passed off as black Americans. In the early 1950s, before mass Commonwealth immigration really got going, black people were mostly seen as a novelty rather than a threat." Williams, "Shirley Bassey." See also Williams, *Miss Shirley Bassey*.

49. Medhurst, "Arts."

50. Medhurst, "Arts."

51. Jose, "One (Wo)man Show."

Chapter 4. From "Ne me quitte pas" to "If You Go Away": Adapting Iconic Songs to Film and Stage

1. Blau and Brel, *Jacques Brel Is Alive and Well*, 40.

2. Benson, "Remember . . . The American Film Theatre!"

3. Tinker, "Jacques Brel Is Alive and Well," 184–85.

4. As Chris Tinker notes, McKuen's versions are "aimed primarily at mainstream domestic audiences" ("Jacques Brel is Alive and Well," 181).

5. Canby, "American Film Theater's."

6. Venuti, "Adaptation, Translation, Critique," 30.

7. Susam-Sarajeva, "Translation and Music," 189.

8. Jellenik, "On the Origins of Adaptation," 41. It's important to note the Western bias in discussions of the origins of adaptation.

9. Mireia Aragay remarks, "The history of adaptation is as long as the history of cinema itself" (*Books in Motion*, 11).

10. Murray, *Adaptation Industry*.

11. Corrigan, "Defining Adaptation," 32.

12. Venuti, "Adaptation, Translation, Critique," 25.

13. Mazdon, *Encore Hollywood*, 27. For a detailed discussion of intertextuality, see Kristeva, *Texte du roman*.

14. Mazdon, *Encore Hollywood*, 27.

15. Maysa Matarazzo, "Maysa—Ne me quitte pas," YouTube, uploaded by stiflerzinha1, https://youtu.be/qP-otWkd8l8?.

16. Quiroga, *"Law of Desire,"* 52.

17. Almodóvar and Strauss, *Almodóvar on Almodóvar*, 72.

18. Almodóvar and Strauss, *Almodóvar on Almodóvar*, 72.

19. Quiroga, *"Law of Desire,"* 93. Almodóvar has called this song "one of the great love songs of all times because it deals with love at a literary level" (92).

20. Interestingly, a later film by Almodóvar, *Mujeres al borde de un ataque de nervios* (Women on the verge of a nervous breakdown) further adapts *La voix humaine*. Almodóvar and Strauss, *Almodóvar on Almodóvar*, 80. Furthermore, Almodóvar has seen his own films be adapted: "Oddly enough, my films have often been turned into plays. This may be due to their rather theatrical dramatic structure, something I hadn't been aware of until I learned they were being re-produced on stage" (81).

21. Quiroga, *"Law of Desire,"* 93.

22. Sasha Velour, "Sasha Velour at Bizarre," YouTube, uploaded by phoneshowz, April 23, 2017, https://youtu.be/X49BMFp7fno?.

23. Quittner, "From Bushwick to (Off-Off) Broadway."

24. Velour uses she/her pronouns when performing and they/them pronouns in their personal life. Quittner, "From Bushwick to (Off-Off) Broadway."

25. Merli, "Urbana Native."

26. Zimmerman, *Women and Other Monsters*.

27. See Judith Butler's *Gender Trouble* and *Bodies That Matter*, 85.

28. Fleisher, *Drag Queens of New York*, 75.

29. Fleisher, *Drag Queens of New York*, 76.

30. Landon, "Sydney's Carnival Queens."

31. Medhurst, "Arts."

32. Claudio Carneiro, "Cirque du Soleil's Varekai—'Ne me quitte pas,'" YouTube, uploaded by truls1ify, November 17, 2011, https://youtu.be/hV9COuYcc9s?.

33. Jones, "Cirque du Soleil's 'Varekai.'"

34. Quezada-Macchiavello, "Interacciones sin nombre," 112.

35. Quezada-Macchiavello, "Interacciones sin nombre," 119–22.

36. "Behind the Curtain."

37. For an exploration of the relationship between Blackness and femininity, see Joseph, *Postracial Resistance*.

38. Johnson, "'Quare' Studies," 5, 10.

39. Johnson, *Appropriating Blackness*, 4.

40. Müller, *Hearing Sexism*, 44.

BIBLIOGRAPHY

Ahmed, Sara. *The Cultural Politics of Emotion*. New York: Routledge, 2004.

Ahmed, Sara. *Queer Phenomenology: Orientations, Objects, Others*. Durham, NC: Duke University Press, 2006.

Alexander, Elizabeth. "'Can You Be Black and Look at This?': Reading the Rodney King Video(s)." *Public Culture* 7, no. 1 (1994): 77–94. https://doi.org/10.1215/08992363-7-1-77.

Almodóvar, Pedro, and Frédéric Strauss. *Almodóvar on Almodóvar*. London: Faber and Faber, 2006.

Aragay, Mireia. *Books in Motion: Adaptation, Intertextuality, Authorship*. Amsterdam: Rodopi, 2005.

Barrett, Lindon. *Blackness and Value: Seeing Double*. Cambridge: Cambridge University Press, 1999.

Bassey, Shirley. *My Life on Record and in Concert*. London: Bloomsbury, 1998.

Bassnett, Susan. *Translation Studies*. 3rd ed. London: Routledge, 2002.

Bedjaoui, Ahmed. "Once upon a Time, There Was PANAF: Liberation Movements and Cultural Representations of African Dreams." *NKA* 1, no. 42/43 (2018): 170–83. https://doi.org/10.1215/10757163-7185821.

"Behind the Curtain: An Interview with JOYÀ's Leading Clown." *Vidanta Traveler*, June 27, 2019. https://magazine.vidanta.com/en/2019/06/27/behind-the-curtain-an-interview-with-joyas-leading-clown/.

Benaglia, Cecilia, and Maya Angela Smith. "Multilingual Texts and Contexts: Inclusive Pedagogies in the French Foreign Language Classroom." In *Diversity and Decolonization in French Studies*, edited by Siham Bouamer and Loïc Bourdeau, 17–32. New York: Palgrave Macmillan, 2022.

Benson, Raymond. "Remember … The American Film Theatre!" *Cinema Retro*, April 16, 2009. https://www.cinemaretro.com/index.php?/archives/3150-REMEMBER…THE-AMERICAN-FILM-THEATRE!.html.

Berruer, Pierre. *Jacques Brel va bien: Il dort aux Marquises*. Paris: Presses de la Cité, 1983.

"The Best of Nina Simone: After 43 Years, Nina Remains Musically Uncategorizable." *Jacksonville Free Press*, December 6, 2000. https://www.proquest.com/newspapers /best-nina-simone-after-43-years -remains-musically/docview/365294218 /se-2.

Bibard, Laurent. *Penser avec Brel*. Paris: L'Harmattan, 2006.

Blau, Eric, and Jacques Brel. *Jacques Brel Is Alive and Well and Living in Paris*. New York: Dutton, 1971.

Borawski, Walta. "For the Love of Nina: Celebrating the Music and Politics of a Great Performer on the Eve of a Rare Boston Visit." *Gay Community News* 19, no. 43/44 (1992): 11. https://www.proquest.com /docview/199357703.

Brand, Dionne. *Bread out of Stone: Recollections, Sex, Recognitions, Race, Dreaming, Politics*. Toronto: Coach House Press, 1994.

Brel, Jacques. *Ne me quitte pas*. Paris: Éditions Musicales Tutti, 1959.

Brooks, Daphne. *Liner Notes for the Revolution: The Intellectual Life of Black Feminist Sound*. Cambridge, MA: Harvard University Press, 2021.

Brooks, Daphne. "Nina Simone's Triple Play." *Callaloo* 34, no. 1 (2011): 176–97. https://muse .jhu.edu/article/418422.

Brun-Lambert, David. *Nina Simone: Une vie*. Flammarion, 2005.

Butler, Judith. *Bodies That Matter: On the Discursive Limits of Sex*. New York: Routledge, 2011.

Butler, Judith. *Gender Trouble: Feminism and the Subversion of Identity*. New York: Routledge, 1990.

Canby, Vincent. "American Film Theater's 'Jacques Brel Is Alive . . .'" *New York Times*, February 25, 1975. https://www.nytimes .com/1975/02/25/archives/american-film -theaters-jacques-brel-is-alive.html.

Charpentreau Simonne, and Jacques Charpentreau. *La chanson*. Paris: Éditions Ouvrières, 1960.

Chorus. Les cahiers de la chanson no. 25: Spécial Jacques Brel. Brezolle, France: Éditions du Verbe, 1998.

Cohn, Dorrit. *The Distinction of Fiction*. Baltimore: Johns Hopkins University Press, 1999.

Cohodas, Nadine. *Princess Noire: The Tumultuous Reign of Nina Simone*. Chapel Hill: University of North Carolina Press, 2002.

Cordier, Adeline. "Chanson and Tacit Misogyny." *Journal of European Popular Culture* 4, no. 1 (2013): 37–49. http://dx.doi.org/10.1386/jepc.4.1.37_1.

Cordier, Adeline. *Post-war French Popular Music: Cultural Identity and the Brel-Brassens-Ferré Myth.* Farnham: Ashgate, 2014.

Corrigan, Timothy. "Defining Adaptation." In *Oxford Handbook of Adaptation Studies*, edited by Thomas Leitch, 23–35. New York; Oxford: Oxford University Press, 2017.

Cortés, Lisa, dir. *Little Richard: I Am Everything.* New York: Magnolia, 2023.

Cristiani, François-René, and Jean-Pierre Leloir. *Trois hommes dans un salon: Brel, Brassens, Ferré.* Paris: Fayard / Éditions du Verbe, 2003.

Davis, Angela Y. *Blues Legacies and Black Feminism: Gertrude "Ma" Rainey, Bessie Smith, and Billie Holiday.* New York: Pantheon, 1999.

D. E. H. "Shirley Bassey Is Tops." *The Stage.* July 25, 1957.

Desblache, Lucile. *Music and Translation: New Mediations in the Digital Age.* London: Palgrave Macmillan, 2019.

Drinker, Henry. "On Translating Vocal Texts." *Musical Quarterly* 2 (1952): 225–40. https://doi.org/10.1093/mq/XXXVI.2.225.

Duponchelle, Valérie. "*Ne me quitte pas* de Jacques Brel, 'la chanson d'un lâche qui plie sous le chagrin.'" *Le Figaro,* January 3, 2016. https://www.lefigaro.fr/musique/2016/01/03/03006-20160103ARTFIG00011--ne-me-quitte-pas-de-jacques-brel-la-chanson-d-un-lache-qui-plie-sous-le-chagrin.php.

Feldstein, Ruth. "'I Don't Trust You Anymore': Nina Simone, Culture, and Black Activism in the 1960s." *Journal of American History* 91, no. 4 (2005): 1349–79. https://doi.org/10.2307/3660176.

Fleisher, Julian. *The Drag Queens of New York: An Illustrated Field Guide.* New York: Riverhead Books, 1996.

Frankowski, Alfred. "Spectacle Terror Lynching, Public Sovereignty, and Antiblack Genocide." *Journal of Speculative Philosophy* 33, no. 2 (2019): 268–81. http://muse.jhu.edu/article/730260.

Gillett, Rachel Anne. *At Home in Our Sounds: Music, Race, and Cultural Politics in Interwar Paris.* Oxford: Oxford University Press, 2021.

Giomi, Andrea. "The Case for an Embodied Approach to Listening: Bodies, Technologies and Perception." *Hybrid* 6 (2019). https://doi.org/10.4000/hybrid.581.

Gorin, François. "Jacques Brel." In *La chanson française, Vol. 4*, edited by Christian Lamet, Florence Trédez, François Gorin, Stan Cuesta, and François Ducray, 215–94. Paris: Éditions Scali, 2007.

Gunkel, David J. *Of Remixology: Ethics and Aesthetics after Remix*. Cambridge, MA: MIT Press, 2016.

Hare, Geoff. "Popular Music on French Radio and Television." In *Popular Music in France from Chanson to Techno: Culture, Identity and Society*, edited by Hugh Dauncey and Steve Cannon, 57–75. Aldershot: Ashgate, 2003.

Hawkins, Peter. *Chanson: The French Singer-Songwriter from Aristide Bruant to the Present Day*. Aldershot: Ashgate, 2000.

Haworth, Rachel. "French *Chanson*." *French Studies* 72, no. 1 (2018): 87–96. https://doi .org/10.1093/fs/knx244.

Haworth, Rachel. "The Singer-Songwriter on Stage: Reconciling the Artist and the Performer." *Journal of European Popular Culture* 4, no. 1 (2013): 71–84. https://doi.org/10.1386 /jepc.4.1.71_1.

Hongre, Bruno, and Paul Lidsky. *Jacques Brel: Chansons*. Paris: Hatier, 1976.

James, Joy. "Resting in Gardens, Battling in Deserts: Black Women's Activism." *The Black Scholar* 29, no. 4 (1999): 2–7. https://www .jstor.org/stable/41068835.

Jellenik, Glenn. "On the Origins of Adaptation, as Such: The Birth of a Simple Abstraction." In *Oxford Handbook of Adaptation Studies*, edited by Thomas Leitch, 36–52. Oxford: Oxford University Press, 2017.

Johnson, E. Patrick. *Appropriating Blackness*. Durham, NC: Duke University Press, 2003.

Johnson, E. Patrick. "'Quare' Studies, or (Almost) Everything I Know about Queer Studies I Learned from My Grandmother." *Text and Performance Quarterly* 21, no. 1 (2001): 1–25. https://doi.org/10.1080 /10462930128119.

Jones, Chris. "Cirque du Soleil's 'Varekai' Whips Audience into Frenzy." *Chicago Tribune*, July 20, 2003. https://www.chicago tribune.com/2003/07/21/cirque-du-soleils -varekai-whips-audience-into-frenzy/.

Jose. "One (Wo)man Show." *Variety,* October 1, 1975.

Joseph, Ralina. *Postracial Resistance: Black Women, Media, and the Uses of Strategic Ambiguity*. New York: New York University Press, 2018.

Judd, Bettina. *Feelin: Creative Practice, Pleasure, and Black Feminist Thought*. Evanston, IL: Northwestern University Press, 2023.

Kelly, Andrew. "Translating French Song as a Language Learning Activity." *Équivalences* 22, no. 1 (1992): 91–112. http://dx.doi.org/10 .3406/equiv.1992.1154.

Kristeva, Julia. *Le texte du roman: Approche sémiologique d'une structure discursive transformationnelle*. The Hague: Mouton, 1970.

Landon, Vincent. "Sydney's Carnival Queens." *The Observer*, April 25, 1999.

Lawrence, Sandra. "The Eurovision." *The Stage*, June 27, 2002.

Lieberman, Jeff L., dir. *The Amazing Nina Simone*. New York: Re-emerging Films, 2015.

Light, Alan. *What Happened, Miss Simone? A Biography*. New York: Crown Archetype, 2016.

Loisy, Stéphane. "Avant-propos." In *Jacques Brel en 40 chansons*, edited by Bruno Brel, Stéphane Loisy, and Baptiste Vignol, 7–11. Paris: Hugo Image, 2018.

Loisy, Stéphane. "Ne me quitte pas." In *Jacques Brel en 40 chansons*, edited by Bruno Brel, Stéphane Loisy, and Baptiste Vignol, 39–43. Paris: Hugo Image, 2018.

Looseley, David. *Popular Music in Contemporary France: Authenticity, Politics, Debate.* Oxford: Berg, 2003.

Low, Peter. "Translating Songs That Rhyme." *Perspectives: Studies in Translation Theory and Practice* 16, no. 1/2 (2008): 1–20. https://doi.org/10.1080/13670050802364437.

Marouani, Charley. Charley Marouani to M. Jolivand, Paris, November 16, 1966.

Maultsby, Portia. "Africanisms in African-American Music." In *Africanisms in American Culture*, edited by Joseph E. Holloway, 185–210. Bloomington: Indiana University Press, 1990.

Mazdon, Lucy. *Encore Hollywood, Remaking French Cinema*. London: BFI, 2000.

McKittrick, Katherine. *Dear Science, and Other Stories*. Durham, NC: Duke University Press, 2021.

M. D. "Shirly Bassey Is a Sensation." *Disc*, February 28, 1959.

Medhurst, Andy. "Arts: Why the Boys Love Bassey." *The Observer*, September 11, 1994. http://link.gale.com/apps/doc/A171391544/AONE.

Merli, Melissa. "Urbana Native, Uni Alum Wins Season 9 of 'RuPaul's Drag Race.'" *News Gazette*, June 27, 2017. https://www.news-gazette.com/news/urbana-native-uni-alum-wins-season-9-of-rupauls-dragrace/article_820d1d07-7d16-5da0-aca2-33a404568565.html.

Mitchell, Robin. *Vénus Noire: Black Women and Colonial Fantasies in Nineteenth-Century France*. Athens: University of Georgia Press, 2020.

Monestier, Martin. *Brel: Le livre du souvenir*. Paris: Tchou, 1979.

Morris, Kasey Lynn, Jamie Goldenberg, and Patrick Boyd. "Women as Animals, Women as Objects: Evidence for Two Forms of Objectification." *Personality and Social Psy-*

chology Bulletin 44, no. 9 (2018): 1302–14. https://doi.org/10.1177/0146167218765739.

Müller, L. J. *Hearing Sexism: Gender in the Sound of Popular Music. A Feminist Approach*. Translated by Manu Reyes. Bielefeld: Transcript, 2022.

Muñoz, José Esteban. *The Sense of Brown*. Durham, NC: Duke University Press, 2020.

Murray, Simone. *The Adaptation Industry: The Cultural Economy of Contemporary Literary Adaptation*. Hoboken, NJ: Taylor and Francis, 2011.

Navas, Eduardo. "The Originality of Copies: Cover Versions and Versioning in Remix Practice." *Journal of Asia-Pacific Pop Culture* 3, no. 2 (2018): 168–87. http://muse.jhu.edu /article/713480.

Neal, Mark Anthony. *What the Music Said: Black Popular Music and Black Public Culture*. New York: Routledge, 1999.

"Nina Simone Reveals: 'Mississippi Goddam' Song 'Hurt My Career.'" *Jet*, March 24, 1986.

Peck, David, Phillip Galloway, and Tom Gulotta, prods. *Nina Simone Live in '65 and '68*. San Diego, CA: Reelin' in the Years Productions / Naxos, 2008, DVD video.

Poole, Sara. *Brel and Chanson: A Critical Appreciation*. Dallas, TX: University Press of America, 2004.

Posner, Rebecca. *Linguistic Change in French*. Oxford: Clarendon, 1997.

"Programme Reviews: And Shirley Bassey Really Does Them Proud." *The Stage and Television Today*, September 20, 1962.

Quezada-Macchiavello, Óscar. "Interacciones sin nombre. Un caso emblemático: Ne me quitte pas (Cirque du Soleil)." *Contratexto*, no. 22 (2014): 109–25. https://doi .org/10.26439/contratexto2014.n022.91.

Quiroga, José. *"Law of Desire": A Queer Film Classic*. Vancouver: Arsenal Pulp Press, 2009.

Quittner, Charles. "From Bushwick to (Off-Off) Broadway: How Sasha Velour Marries Her Night Club Roots with Modern Theatricality." *Culturbot*, March 30, 2019. https:// www.culturebot.org/2019/03/29940/from -bushwick-to-off-off-broadway-how -sasha-velour-marrows-her-night-club -roots-with-modern-theatricality/.

Radano, Ronald. *Lying Up a Nation: Race and Black Music*. Chicago: University of Chicago Press, 2003.

Ramdin, Ron. *Reimaging Britain: 500 Years of Black and Asian History*. London: Pluto, 1999.

"Read Mary J. Blige's Heartfelt Nina Simone Rock Hall Induction Speech." *Rolling Stone*, April 14, 2018. https://www.rollingstone. com/music/music-news/read-mary-j

-bliges-heartfelt-nina-simone-rock-hall
-induction-speech-628982/.

Rigaud, Jacques. *L'exception culturelle: Culture et pouvoirs sous la Ve République*. Paris: B. Grasset, 1995.

Riggan, William. *Pícaros, Madmen, Naïfs, and Clowns: The Unreliable First-Person Narrator*. Norman: University of Oklahoma Press, 1981.

Robine, Marc. *Grand Jacques: Le roman de Jacques Brel*. Paris: Éditions Anne Carrière / Éditions du Verbe (Chorus), 1998.

Ross, Deborah. "Sharp as a Diamond, and a Diva Is Forever." *The Independent* (London), September 15, 1997.

Schudel, Matt. "Rod McKuen, Popular Poet, Singer and Songwriter Who Was a '60s Bard, Dies at 81." *Washington Post*, January 31, 2015.

Scott, Derek B. *German Operetta on Broadway and in the West End, 1900–1940*. Cambridge: Cambridge University Press, 2019.

"Shirley Bassey: British Bombshell Wins New Acclaim in United States." *Ebony*, March 1963.

Simone, Nina, and Stephen Cleary. *I Put a Spell on You: The Autobiography of Nina Simone*. 2nd ed. Cambridge, MA: Da Capo, 2003.

Simone, Nina, and Stephen Cleary. *Ne me quittez pas: Mémoires*. Translated by Mimi Perrin. Paris: Presses de la Renaissance, 1992.

Smith, Maya Angela. *Senegal Abroad: Linguistic Borders, Racial Formations, and Diasporic Imaginaries*. Madison: University of Wisconsin Press, 2019.

Smitherman, Geneva. *Talkin and Testifyin: The Language of Black America*. Detroit: Wayne State University Press, 1986.

Stan. "Shirley Bassey Show." *Variety*, July 8, 1970.

Stein, Jordan Alexander. *Fantasies of Nina Simone*. Durham, NC: Duke University Press, 2024.

Stovall, Tyler. *Paris Noir: African Americans in the City of Light*. Boston: Houghton Mifflin, 1996.

Susam-Sarajeva, Şebnem. "Translation and Music: Changing Perspectives, Frameworks and Significance." *Translator* 14, no. 2 (2008): 187–200. https://doi.org/10.1080/13556509.2008.10799255.

Tillet, Salamishah. "Nina Simone's Time Is Now, Again." *New York Times*, June 19, 2015. http://www.nytimes.com/2015/06/21/movies/nina-simones-time-is-now-again.html.

Tinker, Chris. *Georges Brassens and Jacques Brel: Personal and Social Narratives in Postwar Chanson*. Liverpool: Liverpool University Press, 2005.

Tinker, Chris. "Jacques Brel Is Alive and Well: Anglophone Adaptations of French Chanson." *French Cultural Studies* 16, no. 2 (2005): 179–90. https://doi.org/10.1177 /0957155805053706.

Tinker, Chris. "'One State, One Television, One Public': The Variety Show in 1960s France." *Media History* 14, no. 2 (2008): 223–37. https://doi.org/10.1080 /13688800802176821.

Tolan-Szkilnik, Paraska. *Maghreb Noir: The Militant-Artists of North Africa and the Struggle for a Pan-African, Postcolonial Future*. Stanford, CA: Stanford University Press, 2023.

Toy. "Shirley Bassey Show." *Variety*, October 6, 1976.

Venuti, Lawrence. "Adaptation, Translation, Critique." *Journal of Visual Culture* 6, no. 1 (2007): 25–43. https://doi.org/10.1177 /1470412907075066.

Venuti, Lawrence. "Translation, Community, Utopia." In *The Translation Studies Reader*, edited by Lawrence Venuti, 466–86. New York: Routledge, 2000.

Venuti, Lawrence. *The Translator's Invisibility: A History of Translation*. London Routledge, 1995.

Vincendet, Serge. *Jacques Brel, l'impossible rêve*. Monaco: Alphée Jean-Paul Bertrand, 2008.

Weisbard, Eric. *Hound Dog*. Singles. Durham, NC: Duke University Press, 2023.

Williams, John L. *Miss Shirley Bassey*. New York: Quercus, 2010.

Williams, John L. "Shirley Bassey: From Single Mum to Superstar." *Radio Times*, September 29, 2011. https://www.radiotimes .com/audio/shirley-bassey-from-single -mum-to-superstar/.

Wood, Amy Louise. *Lynching and Spectacle: Witnessing Racial Violence in America, 1890–1940*. Chapel Hill: University of North Carolina Press, 2009.

Yacobi, Tamar. "Package Deals in Fictional Narrative: The Case of the Narrator's (Un) Reliability." *Narrative* 9, no. 2 (2001): 223–29. http://link.gale.com/apps/doc/A75833116 /AONE.

Zimmerman, Jess. *Women and Other Monsters: Building a New Mythology*. Boston: Beacon, 2021.

INDEX